THE ESSENCE OF WON BUDDHISM

THE ESSENCE OF WON BUDDHISM

VENERABLE WOLSAN
VENERABLE YETAWON
REV. DOSUNG YOO

IlWon Publications

The Essence of Won Buddhism

Copyright @ 2024 by IlWon Publications
All rights reserved.
No part of this book may be reproduced in any form without permission in writing from the publisher.

Published by IlWon Publications
361 Route 23, Claverack, NY 12513, USA
Phone: 518-851-2581

Library of Congress Control Number: 2024934104
ISBN: 979-8-9869466-7-2

Illustration by Rev. Semyong Ah
Cover design by Kathy Abeyatunge
Printed in the Republic of Korea

CONTENTS

Translators' Foreword   vii

Chapter 1
Introduction

Sotaesan, the Founding Master of Won Buddhism	3
The Historical Background of Won Buddhism	7
What is Won Buddhism?	10

Chapter 2
The Life of Master Sotaesan

Sotaesan's Birth and Early Childhood	15
Seeking the Way	18
The Great Enlightenment	26
Spreading the Dharma	29
Nirvana	46

Chapter 3
Il-Won-Sang

Discovering Our True Self	57
The Meaning of Il-Won-Sang	62
Il-Won and Il-Won-Sang	66
Faith in Il-Won-Sang	71
The Need for Spiritual Cultivation	78
Practice of Il-Won-Sang	84
The Ultimate Key to Success in Practice	105
Il-Won-Sang and The Goal of Our Life	109

Chapter 4
The View of Birth and Death in Won Buddhism

What is Birth and Death?	117
Preparation for One's Future Life	123
The Grave Matter of Life and Death	167

Afterword	181
Bibliography	185
About the Authors	187
About the Translators	189

Translators' Foreword

One day, when I was working at the Seoul Meditation Center in Korea, one of my fellow ministers paid me a visit. He was very knowledgeable in meditation, chi, and the human body. After observing my sitting meditation posture, he expressed an interest in examining my legs and pelvis. He then instructed me to lie face-down and draw my heels close to my buttocks.

When assessing my legs, he observed that my left leg appeared longer than my right. This was an indication of a slight imbalance in my pelvis. As a result, he advised me to check the heels of my shoes. I found that the left shoe's heel was notably more worn than the right. I usually meditated in a cross-legged position, placing each foot atop the opposite thigh. For many years, I had positioned my right foot over my left thigh and vice versa. Remaining in that position for extended durations eventually resulted in a leftward tilt of my pelvis and resulted in making my left leg appear longer than the right.

He said that our spine is the central support of our body. A misalignment in my pelvis was the source of my lower back discomfort. Furthermore, he mentioned that a potential impact on my kidneys and bladder could occur which could result in these organs becoming compromised.

Much as a robust spine is essential for a physically healthy body, there is a mental counterpart in our life. This mental backbone is our value system, or what we consider most important in our life. Our value system and our life goal direct our desires, thoughts, and priorities.

A high school friend of mine went on to become a Christian pastor. He was diagnosed with cancer during his college years but managed to recover through fasting and prayer. I once inquired if his choice to be a pastor was a way of showing gratitude to God for healing him. His response was very unexpected. He said the main reason he chose that path was because he found eternal life. This was something he hadn't thought about before. Becoming a Christian pastor wasn't just the experience of recovering from his illness or being healed, but his understanding of the Truth. This realization, he said, profoundly transformed his life: his new life goal and values.

Sotaesan, the founding master of Won Buddhism said, ".... the urgent matter at hand is not to teach everyone all the thousands of scriptures or to encourage them to do thousands of good deeds. Rather, the most urgent matter is to first help them believe in and awaken to the truth of neither arising nor ceasing and the karmic principle of cause and effect."

"Neither arising nor ceasing" refers to the truth of eternal life. Yet, how many people truly have a steadfast and authentic faith in eternal life? Furthermore, how many genuinely believe in the karmic principle of cause and effect, the understanding that our actions yield direct consequences?

We can all reshape our mental framework by contemplating what is most significant and imperative in our lives and by adhering to sound practices.

I recall a tale about a deer that cherished its magnificent antlers but despised its unattractive legs. Yet, when pursued by a hunter in the woods, the deer realized that it was those very legs that ensured its survival. In contrast, its prized antlers nearly proved fatal as they became entangled in the tree branches.

When I was in kindergarten, I was enamored with collecting marbles. As I transitioned into elementary school, my passion for them waned. By fourth grade, I had developed a keen interest in collecting postage stamps and dedicated a lot of time and money to that hobby. Yet, that fervor was fleeting and faded as I entered junior high school.

Often, the pursuits and passions we possess during a particular period of time lose their allure as we grow and our values evolve. I found this to be true in my shifting interests from marbles to sports cards and postage stamps. Undoubtedly, many of the things we chase fervently might seem insignificant from the perspective of enlightened sages and buddhas.

Understanding and remembering the truth of eternal life and

the karmic principle of cause and effect will truly reshape our life and our value system. Gaining a fuller understanding of these principles will lead us to reevaluate our life's priorities. Many of the things that often entice us, like fame, elevated social standing, or material wealth, will diminish in importance. By distancing ourselves from these allurements, we pave the way for a more serene and enriched life.

A prophet once lamented, "My people are destroyed for the lack of knowledge of God."

The guiding principle of our lives should be rooted in universal truth. This truth is our original true nature. In Won Buddhism, this is symbolized by a circle, known as Il-Won-Sang. The lives of buddhas and enlightened teachers exemplify this Il-Won-Sang or universal truth.

Chapter 1: Il-Won-Sang and Chapter 2: The Life of Master Sotaesan offer invaluable insight for our life goals and spiritual practice. These two chapters are translations from Venerable Wolsan's book, "Introduction to Won Buddhism" with Reverend Dosung Yoo providing additional explanations and commentaries to enhance the understanding of the work.

I once served at the Won Institute of Graduate Studies. Following our morning meditation, all ministers and pre-ministers undertook the task of cleaning their designated areas. My assignment was the basement of the dormitory, which housed an ancient stone edifice. Every day, descending into that basement, I would find countless centipedes darting across the floor. I'd gently gather them up daily and relocated them outdoors. Yet, every subsequent morning, I would be met with another multitude of centipedes. This routine persisted for a month.

One day, after the morning cleaning, a thought struck me: "If this single building seems to have an infinite number of centipedes, I wonder about the total number worldwide. And considering centipedes are just one species of insect, how vast must the global insect population be? How many fish or other animals populate the world?"

Buddha once said, "Being born as a human is an extraordinary and infrequent occurrence. Having the fortune of a healthy body is even more rare, and the chance to encounter the teachings of the buddhas is the rarest of all." In Buddhist teachings, these are referred to as the 'Three Difficulties.'

Following my encounters with the centipedes, the Buddha's words resonated with me profoundly.

Indeed, being born as a human is an exceptional occurrence, and encountering the Buddhadharma, which guides us towards eternal life, is even more extraordinary.

Sotaesan said, "You meeting me is much like a blind person grabbing hold of a door handle. Now that you have found it, you must continue to hold it firmly. If you are careless and let go, it will not be easy to take hold of again."

We, as practitioners, must profoundly recognize this unique and splendid gift of being born human and encountering the

Buddhadharma. This rarity might be likened to a blind individual happening upon a door handle purely by coincidence.

Since we have encountered the Buddhadharma, we need to make good use of this rare opportunity and pour all our effort into training our mind in order to attain liberation from the suffering of life and death. Embracing this concept is the ultimate direction of our mind practice.

Chapter 3: The View of Birth and Death in Won Buddhism provides detailed guidance for preparing ourselves to transcend the cycle of life and death. Reverend Dosung Yoo adds further explanations and commentaries to ensure a comprehensive grasp of the material presented in this chapter, which is translated from Venerable Yetawon's book, "Getting Familiar with Death," Part 1.

It is our sincere wish and prayer that this book instills in readers a transformative sense of hope for their future and a refreshed perception of their own existence.

Many individuals lent their support in translating "The Essence of Won Buddhism" into English. My heartfelt appreciation goes to Lee Hae-jung who played a pivotal role in crafting significant portions of the preliminary draft. Much of Chapter 4 draws from the translated content of the book, "Getting Familiar with Death" by Venerable Yetawon (Won Publications, 2006). For this fresh translation, I am deeply indebted to and extend my gratitude towards Prof. Park Jin-young for her foundational translation of the book.

    We also owe a deep debt of gratitude to numerous members of the Won Dharma Center. Without their diligent support and adept editing acumen, this endeavor would have remained unfinished.

    May everyone find guidance in the teachings of the buddhas and may all living beings find liberation from suffering.

Reverend Dosung Yoo and Kathy Abeyatunge
Won Dharma Center, 2024

CHAPTER 1

Introduction

Sotaesan
The Founding Master of
Won Buddhism

Sotaesan (1891-1943) is the founding master of Won Buddhism, who was enlightened to the Truth of Il-Won.

Sotaesan was born in 1891 to a peasant family in a small South Korean rural village. From the age of seven, he began to have persistent spiritual questions about nature and human life. He wondered, "How high is the sky?" "Where do the clouds and wind come from?" He questioned everything he observed, and each inquiry led to the next. The more engrossed he became in these countless spiritual questions, the more frustrated he grew because he lacked spiritual guidance.

At the age of eleven, Sotaesan attended a seasonal ceremony for the Remembrance of Ancestors, and there he heard a story about an omniscient mountain spirit. He hoped that meeting such a divine being would provide answers to all his spiritual questions. Every day for five years, Sotaesan walked four kilometers from his home to the Sambat Mountain Pass and prayed to meet the mountain spirit. Yet, he never did, which intensified his frustration.

At the age of sixteen, Sotaesan heard an ancient tale about a person who had achieved enlightenment while practicing under a spiritual guide. For the next six years, he searched for a spiritual guide who could help him find the answers he sought. However, he was unable to find one.

By the time Sotaesan was twenty-two, he had stopped searching for a spiritual guide and instead had became deeply absorbed with one single thought: "What am I supposed to do?" During this time, he often entered deep meditation, forgetting time and place and resting in the genuine realm of stillness.

On April 28th, 1916, after twenty years of searching for the truth, Sotaesan attained great enlightenment. He was twenty-six years old. That day marks the beginning of Won Buddhism.

After his enlightenment, Sotaesan read extensively from the scriptures of numerous religions. Upon reading the Diamond Sutra, he said, "Shakyamuni Buddha is truly the sage of sages. Although I have attained The Way without any teacher's guidance, looking back, from the time of my initial aspiration up to my final enlightenment, many aspects of my experience coincide with the practice and sayings of the Buddha in the past. For this reason, I regard Shakyamuni Buddha as my original teacher and the antecedent of my dharma. In the future, when I establish a religious order, I will create in this world a perfect and complete dharma by taking the teachings of the Buddha as its core."

Sotaesan embraced the main tenets of the Buddha's teaching, but modernized and revitalized the traditional Buddhadharma to make it relevant and accessible to as many people as possible and to enrich their daily lives.

After his enlightenment, many people gathered to become his

disciples and students. This newly created community organized a savings association under Sotaesan's direction.

In April 1918, using the funds, Sotaesan and his followers constructed a levee on a deserted, muddy beach in his hometown of Youngsan. The levee kept the salty sea water at bay and its enclosed twenty-two acres eventually turned into fertile land. Crops were grown and sold to neighboring towns to provide a source of revenue and a means of subsistence for the developing Won Buddhist community.

In 1919, Sotaesan asked his nine disciples to offer a prayer for the deliverance of all beings. Through their selfless and sincere prayer, Won Buddhism received approval from the dharma realm.

From 1920 to 1924, at Bongnae-chongsa Hermitage, Sotaesan created a new dharma so that the followers of his teaching could attain and use the Great Way without leaving their secular lives.

In 1924, Sotaesan founded "The Society for the Study of Buddhadharma," a spiritual community with the mission of liberating all beings from suffering. This community flourished and later became the Headquarters of Won Buddhism, where Sotaesan and his followers worked, practiced, and studied the dharma together under his new vision: "Daily life is Buddhadharma and Buddhadharma is daily life."

For twenty-eight years, Sotaesan worked tirelessly to spread the dharma and save all beings from suffering. On June 1, 1943, he passed away at the age of fifty-three.

Most scriptures from various spiritual traditions are transcriptions of oral transmissions. However, one of the distinguishing features of Won Buddhism is that Sotaesan wrote the Won Buddhist Scriptures himself. Until Sotaesan entered Nirvana, he meticulously edited and recorded his essential teachings, which are compiled in *The Principal Book of Won Buddhism*.

The Historical Background of Won Buddhism

At the time of Sotaesan's birth in 1891, the world was experiencing a surge in colonization. As a result, smaller nations struggled to retain their independence while imperial powers sought to occupy them. Those occupying countries introduced what they termed as "civilized governance" and "modernity." The Korean people, in particular, endured a difficult era. Rife with internal corruption and disagreements among the ruling classes, the nation suffered from oppression, famine, and recurring diseases. This weakened state eventually led to Korea's colonization by Japan in 1910.

During this turbulent chapter in Korean history, many leaders pushed for social and political reform. However, Sotaesan perceived a more pressing matter: addressing the root causes of critical societal issues. He recognized that, alongside the inevitable march of scientific and technological progress, was an essential need to fortify the human mind. He was particularly concerned with the ailment of the human spirit, which was weakened by an overpowering inclination towards materialism. Sotaesan's insights were profound, highlighting the core reasons for civil, political, and social disturbances. He also offered a perspective on where the solution might lie.

The burden of finding a remedy for these issues weighed heavily on Sotaesan, causing him deep emotional unrest. Yet, this very state of agony paved the way for introspection and meditation, which ultimately led him to a solution. Sotaesan encapsulated his belief in the phrase, "With this Great Unfolding of material civilization, Let there be a Great Unfolding of spirituality." During this period, Sotaesan vowed to pursue enlightenment, attain Buddhahood, and deliver all sentient beings from suffering. After attaining great enlightenment, he established a new religion, aiming for the grand salvation of humanity.

The rapid advancement of materialism and consumerism in contemporary society dominates people's minds, making them driven, competitive, and anxious. Sotaesan believed that the way to lead people to a happy life, free from suffering, is by empowering their minds and strengthening their spiritual capacities. This can only be done through faith in truthful dharma and realistic spiritual practice. That is why Won Buddhism emphasizes mind training practice.

In the movie 'Ben-Hur,' there is a dramatic naval battle scene where slaves are toiling beneath the ship's deck. During the battle, the ship experiences extensive damage and starts sinking. The slaves struggle to free themselves from their chains, but only the strong are able to break free and escape.

Just as physical strength allowed those strong slaves to break their physical chains, we need to cultivate our "mental strength" to shatter the various chains of ignorance that bind our minds and lives.

Breaking free and liberating ourselves from the invisible mental shackles of slavery in our lives is a task that all humans must embark upon.

Only through this inner transformation can we forge a path to an expansive and boundless paradise within our lives.

This is the founding motive of Won Buddhism.

What is Won Buddhism?

The name Won Buddhism (*Won-Bul-Kyo* in Korean) is a compound word for truth, enlightenment, and teaching. 'Won' means circle and symbolizes the ultimate truth. 'Bul' means enlightenment, and 'Kyo' means teaching the truth. Therefore, Won Buddhism is the path that leads us to become enlightened to the truth.

Sotaesan (1891-1943) attained great enlightenment in 1916 in Korea after many years of searching for the truth and engaging in many ascetic practices. He embraced the Buddha's teaching, yet he modernized and revitalized the traditional Buddhadharma so that many people in the secular world can utilize it to enrich their everyday lives.

After Sotaesan's great enlightenment, he created the image of Il-Won, also known as "One Circle," which symbolizes ultimate reality. Il-Won represents the origin of the universe and our original nature. All Won Buddhist temples enshrine this Il-Won image at the altar, as an object of faith and the model for practicing Won Buddhist teachings.

Sotaesan observed that humanity was becoming dominated by the rapid development and advancement of material civilization. Thus, he declared the founding motto of Won Buddhism: "With the great unfolding of material developments, let there be a great unfolding of spirituality."

The central teaching of Won Buddhism is the Fourfold Grace, Dharmakaya (Truth) Buddha, which consists of the Grace of Heaven and Earth, the Grace of Parents, the Grace of Fellow Beings, and the Grace of Laws.

The Fourfold Grace is fundamental to our efforts to transform this chaotic world into a peaceful one, as it expresses the interdependence of all beings.

In Won Buddhism, treating every living being as a buddha is an act of faith, as expressed in the motto: "Everywhere a Buddha, Every Act a Buddha Offering."

Won Buddhism teaches us how to use our mind. Everything is of our mind's creation. This is the essence of the Buddha's teaching. Both the state of the world and the state of our lives are manifestations of our mind. Knowing how to use our mind is fundamental and is the key to a happy and fulfilling life. Therefore, mind practice, which teaches how to use the mind, is fundamental to Won Buddhist practice. Sotaesan said, "The study of any science has limits to its use, but if you learn how to make the mind function, this study can be utilized without a moment's interruption. Therefore, mind practice becomes the basis for all other studies." "If the mind is wholesome, everything wholesome arises along with it; if the mind is unwholesome, everything unwholesome arises along with it. Thus, the mind becomes the basis for everything wholesome and unwholesome."[1]

Timeless Meditation, Placeless Meditation is the essential path to mind practice, a way to practice meditation at all times, in every place. It teaches us how to maintain a peaceful, focused state of mind and how to use our original mind efficiently in our daily lives.

Through Sotaesan's vision, traditional Buddhadharma was re-envisioned so that followers of Sotaesan could practice the path to enlightenment without abandoning their secular lives. Sotaesan said, "We do not want to be useless to the world because we are buddhist practitioners. Rather, we want to become very useful to our families, society, and our nation through the practical application of the Buddhadharma." Won Buddhism welcomes and embraces all people and all traditions of other faiths and strives to establish a World of Oneness in which all people live in harmony. With its open and inclusive teachings, Won Buddhism is working to realize the vision of United Religions as a counterpart to the United Nation.

---

1. *The Scriptures of Won-Buddhism*, 355.

Chapter 2

The Life of Master Sotaesan

Sotaesan's Birth and Early Childhood

Sotaesan (1891-1943), the founding master of Won Buddhism, was enlightened to the Truth of Il-Won and established Won Buddhism in Korea.

Born in 1891 to a peasant family in a small South Korean village, he was a conscientious and magnanimous boy who carefully observed all natural phenomena. He also held great respect for his elders and took pleasure in asking them about their lives. Having an unwavering commitment to upholding the promises he made, Sotaesan was able to be steadfast and focused when faced with challenging situations.

Sotaesan's character is quite aptly illustrated in recounting two incidents from when he was just four years old.

In the late spring of 1896, in the small town of Youngchon where Sotaesan was born, the whole village was in a state of anxiety over the impending approach of the Donghak Revolutionary Army which was under the command of General Chun Bong-Jun. The Donghak Army was composed of disgruntled peasants who held resentment towards the corrupt and exploitative practices of government authorities. Much of the population was afraid of the Donghak Revolutionary Army because thieves and rioters who often disguised themselves as Revolutionary soldiers. This band of soldiers killed and pillaged villages throughout the land. The adults in Sotaesan's life spoke about these events, and he listened very carefully.

One morning, Sotaesan was having breakfast with his father, Park Sung-sam, at their home in Norumok. Observing that his bowl had less rice compared to his father's, Sotaesan he took some rice from his father's bowl. His father light-heartedly admonished him, "You took from my bowl without asking, so you deserve to be punished." Sotaesan responded playfully by saying "If you decide to punish me, I'll surprise you first." Sotaesan's father was amused and did not pay much attention to Sotaesan's words.

After the meal, Park Sung-sam was resting in his room when all of a sudden Sotaesan shouted: "The Donghak Army is coming to Norumok! The Donghak Revolutionary Army is here!"

Park Sung-sam was so frightened by his son's shouting that he ran out of the room without even his shoes, and hid in the bamboo grove behind their house. After some time had passed, Sotaesan's mother decided to take a look around the village, but she found no sign of the Donghak army anywhere. When she returned home, she asked Sotaesan whether or not the Donghak Army had actually come to Norumok. Sotaesan responded, "No, I just wanted to keep my word about surprising Father!" As such, since he was very young, he was determined to keep all the promises that he made, even if the circumstances were absurd.

Then, one summer day, when Sotaesan was five years old, he was playing in a creek near the village with his friends. His friends suddenly became very frightened, and some even burst out crying. Sotaesan stopped and asked his friends why they were so upset. With their hands trembling, the two other children pointed to a large snake lying in the grass nearby. Little Sotaesan approached the snake with a stick in his hand and shouted, "You mean snake! How dare you scare my friends!" In response to his loud shouting, the snake turned its head and slithered away into the bushes.

As such, little Sotaesan's boldness was often exhibited in his youth, and so people in his village called him the "small but bold child."

Seeking the Way

Questions Arise while Looking at the Sky.

At the early age of seven, Sotaesan grew deeply interested in the universal truths manifested in nature.

One day, he looked up at the clear sky and out at the surrounding mountains, which were filled with pure, clear energy. Suddenly, questions arose in his mind: "The sky is so high and vast, how did it become so clear?" and "How do the winds and clouds arise so unexpectedly from these clear skies?"

Filled with extraordinary curiosity, his mind continued to give rise to questions such as these. From the age of nine, he began to look inward and reflect deeply. Thus, his own existence became the subject of his contemplation.

Seeking the answers to all life's questions became the focus of his every waking hour. When he thought of his parents and his siblings, questions arose about them too. When he observed the change of day to night, that then became the object of his inquiry. His own incessant questioning left him often deeply restless and frustrated.

Searching for a Mountain Spirit

Sotaesan's parents sent him to a private Confucian school, but he did not concentrate on his studies. He was disinterested in playing with the other children and was only focused on solving the questions that arose in his mind. When Sotaesan was eleven years old, his family took him to an ancestral ritual at a mountain village, Maup. Sotaesan noted that they first performed a ceremony for a mountain spirit before holding the ancestral ritual. He asked one of his relatives, "Why do we have the mountain spirit ceremony before the ancestral rituals?"

The family member explained to him that the mountain spirit governs the mountain due to their immense power and omniscience. Upon hearing this, Sotaesan's enthusiasm surged, and he inquired if he could encounter the mountain spirit to seek answers to his myriad of questions. The relative responded affirmatively but emphasized that he would have to commit wholeheartedly and single-mindedly to the quest.

So, seeking the mountain spirit, Sotaesan trekked up Sambat Pass to offer his prayers. This modest mountain, located close to his residence, was two and a half miles away. Every single morning, he undertook this journey without informing his parents. During this time period, numerous wild tigers roamed the mountains, deterring even the bravest of adults.

Nonetheless, little Sotaesan remained resolute. Every day, he ascended Sambat Pass to offer prayers at Court Rock in hopes of encountering the mountain spirit. He also presented fruit offerings and reverently bowed in all four directions. Young Sotaesan often did not head home until after the sun had set. There were even instances when he'd drift off to sleep at the base of Court Rock, only to awaken at dawn.

For five years, he maintained this ritual, never skipping a day, no matter the challenges or adverse weather. One day, when his mother discovered his relentless excursions to the mountain, she was profoundly touched by his dedication and earnestness. So, she supported Sotaesan's quest to learn all the mysteries of the universe.

Even though Sotaesan prayed faithfully for five years at Sambat Pass, he was never able to the mountain spirit.

At the age of fifteen, Sotaesan's father, Park Sung-sam, set up a marriage for him with Yang Ha-un, hoping that this would deter Sotaesan from his quest for enlightenment. Sotaesan married Yang Ha-un. However, Sotaesan's spiritual journey remained undeterred.

The next year, as he reached the age of sixteen, Sotaesan attended a New Year's celebration with his in-laws. During the gathering, he overheard tales of how Taoist sages achieved spiritual enlightenment through encounters with esteemed masters. This discussion of *The Story of Paktaebo* and *The Story of Cho-ung* inspired Sotaesan to seek wisdom directly from a great master. Upon returning home, he set his mind on following a different path. Although he was still determined to obtain the answers he sought, he let go of his fruitless search for the mountain spirit. Instead, he turned his mind toward meeting a sage. He thought to himself, "I have not seen the mountain spirit in these five years, despite all my effort and devotion. Therefore, I cannot be certain if the mountain spirit even exists. However, if I make an effort to search for a sage, like the characters in the stories, I should be able to discover one."

After returning home from his in-laws, Sotaesan put all his effort into finding his spiritual master.

Searching for His Spiritual Master

From the tales Sotaesan gleaned from his in-laws', these spiritual masters were described as having immense supernatural abilities, akin to deities. It was also said that locating them was a challenge because they could easily blend in and may appear as a mere ordinary beggar. Consequently, Sotaesan began investigating every beggar he encountered on the streets, and tried to determine if any of them were, in fact, revered spiritual masters.

One day, Sotaesan passed a beggar sitting in front of the entrance to a bar, who was reading a Chinese poem. The man said in a loud voice, "Who will awaken first from this deep dream?!" Intrigued and suspecting that this man might be a master, Sotaesan extended an invitation for dinner at his home. However, after engaging in a lengthy conversation, Sotaesan discerned that the man was simply an ordinary individual.

However, Sotaesan continued to seek the truth. Seeing this, his father Park Sung-sam began to support him on his spiritual journey to find a great master.

One day, a self-proclaimed master appeared in the village. When Sotaesan invited him to his family's home, the man said he would answer all of Sotaesan's questions under two conditions. First, Sotaesan should regard him as a great master and treat him with appropriate respect and courtesy. Second, he would receive an ox as payment for answering Sotaesan's questions.

Sotaesan and his father felt that if this master were able to answer Sotaesan's questions, it would be worth the price of an ox.

When they agreed, the "master" began to pray for two days and nights. He said that he was calling his guardian angel who would come to answer Sotaesan's questions. Unfortunately, the prayer did not work, and so the embarrassed "master" requested several more offerings from Park Sung-sam so that he could call upon his guardian angel with even more devotion. Despite all his effort and prayer, the angel did not appear even after three days. So, the man fled in the middle of the night.

In the subsequent years, Sotaesan dedicated considerable time and resources in pursuit of a spiritual master, but to no avail. At the age of twenty, Sotaesan faced the abrupt loss of his caring and encouraging father. This tragedy deeply impacted him. As he persevered in his quest for enlightenment, he now bore the added burden of providing for his family. He felt compelled to settle the debts his father had acquired while he supported Sotaesan's spiritual journey. Taking the advice of his uncle's friend, Sotaesan opened a seasonal fish market on the Imjado and Tari Islands to make money. The markets proved to be a success. This endeavor helped Sotaesan pay back the debts. Still his spiritual questions loomed in his mind, and his desire to find the truth only grew deeper.

What am I supposed to do?

At the age of twenty-two, Sotaesan gave up searching for a spiritual guide who would answer the many questions which had plagued him from an early age. Instead, all his thoughts came together to formulate one single question, "What am I supposed to do?" He was deeply absorbed by this question day and night. Due to this ceaseless preoccupation, his daily life became more difficult, and he often looked like a man who was lost and without direction.

During this time, Sotaesan frequently entered into deep meditation. Time and place did not exist there and he began resting in the genuine realm of stillness. Sotaesan would stop while walking and sit like a stone. It was as if he was lost, unaware of himself or his surroundings.

These meditative states continued for a couple of years.

One early morning, Sotaesan waited for a ferry at Sonjin Landing to go to the market across the river. While waiting, he entered into great Samadhi and stood in absolute calmness until the sun had set.

As people made their way home from the market at dusk, they stumbled upon Sotaesan, standing motionless. They exclaimed, "Hey, Sotaesan! Why are you still here?!" Startled by their calls, Sotaesan woke up.

Sotaesan frequently found himself profoundly engrossed in pondering, "What is my purpose?" His concentration was such that he'd stand motionless on the road for extended periods of time. He remained oblivious to his surroundings. He would often suffer sunburns from being exposed to the intense summer sun for hours on end.

One day, his wife prepared breakfast for him in the early morning before she went out to the field to work. When she returned home around lunch time, she discovered Sotaesan still sitting silently at the breakfast table, absorbed in deep meditation. Even though countless flies buzzed around his bowl of rice, he remained undisturbed.

From the age of twenty-five, the single thought "What am I supposed to do?" began to disappear, and he entered into a deeper samadhi. During this time, he began to develop an intermittent cough, and an abscess formed on his skin. His body also broke out into a rash due to the excessive sun exposure he received.

When neighbors saw Sotaesan in such a state, they were reluctant to approach him as they thought he might have a contagious disease. By most, he was considered insane due to the state of his appearance and his samadhi experiences. Thus, people not only avoided his presence, but also his home. Furthermore, Sotaesan's house was also in great need of repair, causing his family circumstances to become more difficult.

The Great Enlightenment

In the early morning hours of April 28, 1916, Sotaesan sat in deep meditation. As he meditated in his house in Norumok village, his mind and heart suddenly became refreshed and open. By daybreak, his mind had completely cleared.

He immediately left his room and looked out into the clear starlit sky of dawn, and felt a sensation unlike any he had experienced before. Strolling through the courtyard near his house, he reflected on the hardship of previous years. Sotaesan, then, felt the need to comb his hair and cut his nails. He carefully washed his face and when the sun began to shine brightly, he searched for something he could use to clean his body. Once finished, he saw the state of his home and felt the same need to clean what was disheveled and fix everything in need of repair.

At this time, the boils on his body began to disappear as well, revealing clear and smooth skin. After eating breakfast, Sotaesan overheard a discussion between a few neighbors regarding the contents of the *Tong-kyong Taejon* (Great Canon of Eastern Learning), which states: "I, the Heavenly Lord, have a sacred amulet. Its name is Miraculous Medicine, and its form is the Great Circle." Immediately, upon hearing this passage, Sotaesan clearly understood its meaning.

Later, two Confucian scholars passed by Sotaesan's house. They took rest there and discussed a passage in the I-Ching, the Chinese philosophy book: "A great person is united with the virtue of Heaven and Earth, the brightness of the sun and the moon, the sequence of the four seasons, and unified with the good and ill-fortune of the spirit." When Sotaesan heard this passage, he also understood its meaning with perfect clarity.

Sotaesan recalled all the doubts and questions he had previously raised and realized their meaning with the same perfect clarity. He felt inexpressible joy. He had finally achieved great enlightenment.

After his great enlightenment, Sotaesan expressed his state of mind in a verse: "When the moon rises as a fresh breeze blows, the myriad of forms become naturally clear."

Sotaesan also declared, "All beings are of a single nature and all things originate from one source. The Truth of neither arising nor ceasing and the karmic principle of cause and effect operate in perfect harmony, in an interrelated system."

This was his first dharma instruction—the truth to which he had awakened.

This means that the principle of the universe is fundamentally one: the permanent aspect of universal truth or eternal life, is inseparable from the impermanent aspect of universal truth, which is the karmic principle of cause and effect. Together, these elements form a unified reality.

Sotaesan realized that our primal awareness, our universal

consciousness, is everlasting, and all things are continuously changing. Whatever goes, comes again. Whatever comes, goes again. Those who give will receive, and those who receive will eventually give.

However, this awakening was not limited to Sotaesan's own personal experience. His awakened mind and heart became filled with great empathy and compassion. Sotaesan, as a result, sought to reach out with helping hands in order to deliver all sentient beings from suffering.

Spreading the Dharma

Gathering Disciples

Following his enlightenment, Sotaesan underwent a profound transformation. He exuded virtue and compassion like never before. His demeanor carried immense grace, and a luminous radiance surrounded him. This striking change drew individuals towards him, and within a few months, he had amassed a following of forty people.

In 1917, one year after Sotaesan attained great enlightenment, he devised a method to organize his followers in a manner to teach people effectively. This method is referred to as the Kyohwa-dahn, which is the dharma study/practice group that consists of nine members and one leader.

Sotaesan became the leader of the first Kyohwa-dahn. He selected eight disciples who had sincere and strong faith. The first disciples were: Lee Jae-chol, Lee Sun-sun, Kim Ki-chon, Oh Chang-gon, Park Se-chol, Park Dong-guk, Yu Keon, Kim Kwang-son.

However, Sotaesan left the position for the central member vacant. He said "There is a certain person meant for this position.

That person will come soon and help us greatly."

After the Kyohwa-dahn was created, Sotaesan made a mindfulness journal book named, *Sungye-myongshi-rok* and suggested that the disciples spend ten days writing down what and how they have studied and practiced. Thus, they examined the strengthening or weakening of their faith, as well as how they put their faith into action. Initially, this practice evoked a blend of apprehension and intrigue among them. However, they soon recognized that the act of journaling helped immensely to fortify their faith and commitment. The disciples held steadfast belief in Sotaesan's teachings and followed him with profound dedication.

One day, Sotaesan encouraged his disciples to create a savings association, stating, "For us to study and engage in spiritual practice, we must unite and generate income." So, this newly created community followed his direction and organized the savings association. To establish a new religious order, the savings association provided a base of financial support to prepare for future dharma work.

Establishing a Savings Association

In order to save money for this great undertaking, each of Sotaesan's followers made an effort to abstain from drinking alcohol and smoking tobacco. They also worked on holidays and saved the extra income. Additionally, they saved some money by ending expensive memorial rituals which were traditionally offered to the realm of truth. The disciples' wives also helped by saving a small portion of rice, called 'gratitude rice'. All these efforts paved the way for establishing a financially secure community for spiritual practice.

This also served as a way to open and empower their minds and hearts for spiritual awakening and to change the difficult circumstance of their lives under Japanese rule.

Subsequently, Sotaesan recommended using their accumulated savings, along with borrowed funds from an affluent neighbor and money he obtained from selling his household furniture, to buy charcoal. A few months later, during World War I, the demand for charcoal surged, causing its price to skyrocket. Consequently, within a year, the community savings association garnered significant wealth, yielding a profit that was a tenfold increase from their initial expectations.

Having a great sense of responsibility for the money, Sotaesan said, "With the money we have earned together, we can now carry out an important project which I've had in mind. Please listen and contemplate this."

Pointing to the riverside, Sotaesan said "Look at that tidal land! That piece of land has been deserted for a long time, but we could build a dam and transform that tidal land into a rice field. It will take several years to complete, but it will surely strengthen our community as well as our country. Let us start this project for the benefit of the public's welfare."

Embankment Project

The proposal from Sotaesan to construct an embankment at Youngsan surprised them. No one in thousands of years had ever conceived of such an endeavor.

The disciples showed an unwavering faith in Sotaesan and decided to unite and carry out the reclamation project.

This event marked a pivotal chapter both in Won Buddhism and the annals of religious history. No religious faction had ever undertaken such an initiative before. This took place three years after Sotaesan's enlightenment.

When the embankment project began, Sotaesan went out to sea and measured the depth required to drive the posts securely in place. Then the disciples connected the posts with straw ropes to establish the area of the dam. Next, Sotaesan asked his followers to cut pine trees and bring them over to the seashore to build the levee.

This project began only a few months after the savings association had started, yet, the embankment project was remarkably efficient.

Still, the project's execution was fraught with challenges. The magnitude of the task was unprecedented for the villagers. Many mocked the laborers and voiced their profound doubts.

One day, a member of a nearby religious group, who was the brother of Sotaesan's friend, mocked them, saying, "When our teaching has been widely spread, it would be easy to give you the position of local governor. So, it would be better to stop this construction and simply donate the money to our local church instead."

Yet, some of the local people were very supportive and offered words of encouragement. One such person stood up to the naysayers and said, "My dear fellows, don't speak that way. After seeing Sotaesan create the savings union and run the charcoal business, I am certain that it is quite possible for this project to become a success."

As the construction advanced, financial constraints became a hurdle. Faced with this challenge, Sotaesan found himself seeking external sources from which to borrow the necessary funds.

One day, Sotaesan told his disciple, Kim Ki-chon to pay a visit to Kim Deok-il, a rich man in the village, to borrow money. Kim Deok-il was a well-known loan shark and a miser, who never loaned money without a guarantee and good return on his investment. Kim Ki-chon said to Sotaesan, "He will never loan us the money without security. It's just not possible." Sotaesan said, "Go meet with him. He will be happy to give us the loan."

Kim Ki-chon followed Sotaesan's instruction, and visited Kim Deok-Il even though he had some doubts and uncertainty. When Kim Ki-chon asked for the loan, much to his surprise, Kim Deok-il was happy to offer the money. It was as if he had been waiting for him. The very next day he came to the embankment site with the money he had promised.

On April 26, 1919, a year after its commencement, the

embankment project came to fruition. Despite facing numerous challenges and enduring persistent critique, the order successfully transformed around 25 acres of tidal territory into arable farmland. Sotaesan named this farmland *Chongwanpyong*, which translates as "the land for reflecting on purity and righteousness."

This farmland became the economic foundation of the initial stage of Won Buddhism. While the embankment project was at the peak of its construction, Song Kyu, who later became the second Head Dharma Master of Won Buddhism, arrived to join the order.

For an extended period, Sotaesan had keenly anticipated Song Kyu's arrival. Upon his entry, Song Kyu assumed a pivotal role within the Kyohwa-dahn, the dharma study and practice group. Later, they built the first temple at the foot of Ongnyo Peak and named it *Gugwan-dosil*, meaning "nine-room house."

Relying on the Will of Universal Truth

In March 1919, precisely when the embankment project was nearing completion, Korea witnessed a non-violent uprising against Japanese colonization. Known as the March 1st Independence Movement, this protest rapidly gained traction across the nation. Many of Sotaesan's disciples felt compelled to participate in the demonstrations.

When some of his disciples asked Sotaesan, "What should we do at this time?" Sotaesan replied, "This is the sound that resonates, the call for the Great Unfolding of the future. It is the voice of people wishing for a new world. Let us hurry to finish the embankment project and pray for this world."

During this time, Sotaesan had a grander vision in mind. It was to deliver all sentient beings through the Buddhadharma. However, in order to accomplish this, he needed to first obtain dharma authentication from the realm of truth.

Sotaesan told his disciples, "It is our responsibility to prepare ourselves so that we can help deliver all people from suffering. His disciples followed his direction and set out to pray with utmost sincerity and devotion. They first prepared themselves by washing and purifying their body and mind. Then they climbed to the peaks of the Kusu Mountains which Sotaesan had designated for them.

On April 28, the three-year anniversary of Sotaesan' great enlightenment, they began praying. This was also the same day the embankment project was completed. Thereafter, they prayed three times a month, and for the nine following days they did their best to live with a pure mind and heart in accordance with the prayer they offered.

On prayer days, they all gathered in the dharma room of the nine-room house where they received instructions from Sotaesan. They then departed for their designated prayer sites. Each member was given a watch so that they could synchronize their prayer time, and each was assigned a mountaintop as the site of their prayer. At the peak of the mountains, each member carefully arranged his prayer site by setting up a flag at their respective location, preparing incense and a bowl of clear water, bowing, reading the prayer, and reciting a chanting phrase.

The prayer offered was as follows:

I, offer this prayer wholeheartedly to the Fourfold Grace: the Grace of Heaven and Earth, the Grace of Parents, the Grace of Fellow Beings, and the Grace of Laws.
Human beings are the masters of all things; all things should be utilized by human beings. The Way of humanity is grounded on benevolence and righteousness, while deceptive tactics are erroneous. Therefore, it is appropriate that the human spirit naturally utilize all material things and establish the great Way of benevolence and righteousness throughout the world. Currently, however, benevolence and righteousness have lost their influence, and deceptiveness has claimed dominion over the world. As a consequence, establishing the great Way has become fraught with obstacles. Now is the time when we must join our minds and hearts together and act in concert to rectify both the ways of the world and the human mind, which are declining day by day.
We hope and pray that we will uphold the sacred intention and aspiration of Sotaesan and solidify the dharma connection between ourselves and our community. We vow that the right dharma will be established to rectify the declining human spirit.

We sincerely ask the Fourfold Grace to respond to our prayers and to help us accomplish our goal with its boundless power and infinite grace.

This prayer was offered from 10:00 pm until 12:00 am. Afterwards, everyone returned to the nine-room house.

After three months of prayer, Sotaesan said to his disciples, "The devotion and sincerity with which you have prayed is truly praiseworthy. However, I can see that it is not sufficient to move the realm of truth. This is because there still remains some defilement of ego left in your minds. If extinguishing your ego can help establish the correct dharma, will you carry out that task?" To this, the nine disciples said in unison, "Yes, we will."

Sotaesan continued more solemnly, "There's an age-old adage that says, 'To uphold one's virtue and to manifest benevolence, one must sometimes sacrifice oneself for a noble cause.' There have been those who achieved wonders by embracing this tenet. When one dedicates their life to the betterment of all living beings, how could the divine spirits of Heaven and Earth remain unmoved? Soon, a great Way grounded in the true dharma will flourish across the globe, rectifying the misguided perceptions of humanity. This shift will contribute a multitude of blessings to all sentient beings. Then, you will naturally become the saviors of the world, and your merit will become eternal. Therefore, truthfully express your views on this matter from your heart."

The nine disciples were downcast for a while, but in the end, they agreed wholeheartedly that they were willing to sacrifice their lives. With great admiration, Sotaesan highly praised them, and asked them to carry out the sacrifice at their designated prayer sites. This was to take place on the next prayer day, following the ten days of ablutions.[1]

On August 21, the nine disciples gathered in the dharma room, and at 8:00 pm Sotaesan asked them to arrange a bowl of clear water and place their daggers on the table. Also, on the table was a white sheet of paper on which was written their names and the words, "Sacrifice with no Regret." Sotaesan then asked each of them to press their bare thumb underneath their name to symbolize their signature. They were then asked to prostrate and offer a silent prayer affirming their determination to sacrifice their lives on behalf of all sentient beings. When finished, the disciples pressed their bare thumbs on the white paper.

Soon after, Sotaesan examined the paper, and saw that the places where the disciples had pressed their bare thumbs had turned into blood-stained fingerprints. Showing the paper to his disciples, he said, "Look at this paper. This is evidence of your single devoted heart and mind." He then burned the paper to consecrate it to the realm of truth and ordered his disciples to go to their prayer sites.

However, once they stepped out of the dharma room, Sotae-

---

1. *The Scripture of Wonbulkyo*, 1054-1055.

san called them back saying that he had one more thing to tell them. "The spirits of heaven and earth have already responded to your vow. The planning in the realm of dharma has now been completed. The success of our plan has been assured by your action. Your sacrifice has been acknowledged by the world." Hearing Sotaesan's words, the joy and excitement of the disciples could not be quelled for some time.

At 11:00 that night, Sotaesan asked the nine disciples to go to the top of Jung-ahng mountain to offer prayers. When they returned, Sotaesan assigned each of them a dharma name and a dharma title, saying, "The individual who held a secular name has died. Now I give you a new name. With this universal dharma name, you are reborn. I have called you back to life by bestowing on you this name for use throughout the world. Receive and cherish your dharma name with honor and try to deliver numerous sentient beings."

Hence, Sotaesan revitalized the spirits of the nine disciples. Through their willingness to sacrifice for the greater good, he ingrained a deep truth in them: *The purpose of our lives is to serve the well-being of all.*

The transformation of the nine disciples' fingerprints into blood seals is termed "the Event of Dharma Authentication." It was this significant act that granted Won Buddhism its dharma validation from the domain of universal truth. Today, the Day of Dharma Authentication stands as one of the four major annual observances in Won Buddhism.

Since the original nine disciples received their dharma names and dharma titles on this day, receiving a dharma name or dharma title has become a symbol of rebirth from a single secular being into a public figure. Adopting a dharma name signifies a commitment to the path of dharma. This act symbolizes an individual's renewed dedication to pursuing great enlightenment, aiming for the betterment of all living beings.

Creating Dharma for Future Generations

After the event of dharma authentication, Sotaesan asked his disciple, Song Kyu, to go to Zen Master Hakmyong (1867~1929) who resided at Wolmyong Hermitage. Master Hakmyong was a well-known and prominent Zen Master. Sotaesan wanted Song Kyu to become Hakmyong's attendant.

As Song Kyu was leaving, Sotaesan said, "Don't read Buddhist scriptures." Reflecting on this later, Song Kyu mentioned, "I adhered to Sotaesan's guidance and even made an effort to steer clear of the table where the scriptures were kept."

After sending off Song Kyu, Sotaesan began residing in Silsangsa Temple, which was one mile from Wolmyong Hermitage. As more disciples came to see him, they decided to build a thatched cottage for Kim Nam-chon and Song Jeok-byok. That residence was officially known as Bongaejeonsa, but was commonly called "Sukdu-am" Hermitage.

When Sotaesan first began his stay at Sukdu-am Hermitage, he told Song Kyu to terminate his service as the attendant to Master Hakmyeong and return to him. Together with his disciples, Sotaesan began to formulate the core tenets of Won Buddhism, aiming to relieve all sentient beings from their anguish. For about five years prior to the establishment of the Won Buddhism Headquarters, he resided at Bongnae-chongsa Hermitage, where he continued to develop and refine his teachings to aid in the liberation of all beings from their suffering.

The outline of Sotaesan's new teaching was two-pronged: "The Essential Way of Human Life," encompassing "the Fourfold Grace" and "the Four Essentials," and "the Essential Way of Practice," incorporating "the Threefold Practice" and "the Eight Articles." These teachings offered a refreshed and modernized interpretation of traditional Buddhadharma, which allowed adherents to grasp and embody the Great Way without abandoning their everyday lives.

Construction of Headquarters

Sotaesan traveled to Byeonsan, driven by two main objectives. First, he aimed to craft a modern dharma suited for contemporary society. Secondly, he sought to build strong connections and relationships with a vast number of individuals.

While Sotaesan spent five years at Bongnae-chongsa Hermitage, numerous individuals from various regions sought him out in their quest for enlightenment. Later, when it came time for Sotaesan to found the Headquarter, several of these visitors became instrumental in shaping the foundational practice community. Among them was a follower named Seo Jungan. Although he was ten years older than Sotaesan, Seo Jung-an sincerely asked, "Please allow me to call you father." Such a request was unusual, so Sotaesan felt uncomfortable and refused. But, with heartfelt insistence, Seo Jung-an pleaded with Sotaesan to change his mind.

One day, when Seo Jung-an visited Sotaesan at Bongnae Mountain, he made a very important observation, saying, "The road in this area is too rocky and this hermitage is too small. In my humble opinion, you should move to an area that is more easily accessible and has adequate space. This would make it far easier to help guide people in the future." Sotaesan then sensed that the time had come for him to create a new spiritual community, which would be the first step in opening a new religious practice. Thus, he agreed with Seo Jung-an and consented to move his residence.

On June 1, 1914, a meeting was held at Bokwang Buddhist Temple in Iksan to form The Society for the Study of Buddhadharma (later renamed Won Buddhism). From that day, The Society for the Study of Buddhadharma was established in the Shin-rong district in Iksan as a spiritual community where all Sotaesan's followers worked, studied and practiced dharma together. The city of Iksan's convenient location along a central traffic route made the community more accessible.

In November, they constructed two wooden huts with thatched roofs, which marked the beginning of the new spiritual community. However, after erecting these structures, the community faced significant financial challenges. To generate funds, they started a taffy business. They also adopted frugal measures, often subsisting on acacia leaves or taffy rice. Moreover, they took on roles as tenant farmers, leasing modest pieces of land to grow crops and fruit trees.

One day, the renowned freedom fighter Ahn Chang-ho, who had recently been released from prison for his role in the Korean independence movement, visited The Society for the Study of Buddhadharma. Sotaesan warmly welcomed him, commending him for the sacrifices he had made for the Korean people.

Ahn Chang-ho said, "What I am doing is small in scope and short in skill, bringing little benefit to the nation and even leading to the persecution of many of my comrades by the colonial police. But what you, sir, are doing is vast in scope and proficient in its expedience, as you contribute greatly to this cause without anyone being persecuted or put under restraint. How I truly admire your ability!"

Given that Ahn Chang-ho was under surveillance by the Japanese police, he kept his conversation with Sotaesan short. Still, however, after his visit, the local police intensified their monitoring of The Society for the Study of Buddhadharma. The Japanese officials sought to dismantle the newly formed spiritual community. As part of their strategy, they set up a police substation within the Headquarters and secretly placed an undercover officer within the Won community. They meticulously monitored The Society's activities around the clock, sending police and detectives to Headquarters in search of any illicit activities. However, their internal investigation did not find any proof of illegal acts being committed. Sotaesan was also summoned several times to the police station for interrogation. Despite all the hardships, he continued to pour a great deal of effort into training his followers to become seasoned practitioners and great dharma teachers.

By 1924, Sotaesan had established the spiritual community at Shinyong, Iksan; there he worked ceaselessly until his death. He worked with great dedication and sincerity to help alleviate suffering for all people. Sotaesan emphasized that a living religion or practice should not be separate from our daily lives. The essence of his teaching was "Buddhadharma is Daily Life, Daily Life is Buddhadharma."

In 1925, Sotaesan conducted the first meditation retreat based on the newly established method of dharma practice. Due to the limited size of the houses available at the Headquarters at that time, he temporarily rented a space in Jeon Eumkwang's home. This space was used to conduct summer meditation sessions. Approximately ten male and female members participated in these retreats, and were guided by Song Kyu. Song Kyu later would become Sotaesan's dharma successor.

In November, a winter meditation retreat was held for approximately twenty male and female members. This retreat was directed and guided by Lee Chun-pung. These two meditation retreats were the beginning of what would eventually be regarded as the regular dharma retreats for Won Buddhism.

Through such trainings or retreats, Sotaesan refined his new dharma to open the minds and hearts of all suffering people and to deliver all sentient beings.

Such regular retreats not only served as important periods for lay members to train themselves in the study and practice of the dharma, but also served as the only means to train the ministers in the early days of Won Buddhism. A community hall was later constructed and used as the place of training.

Nirvana

Preparation for His Passing

For several years before his death, Sotaesan would often say to his students, "I will leave soon for self-cultivation. Reflect on whether or not you will regress in my absence. Fortify your minds."

When he spoke, his students did not think that he was referring to his impending death. Instead, some thought to themselves, "Sotaesan is a true and great sage, free from birth and death. We will follow him, wherever he goes."

In the Great Enlightenment Hall on January 28, 1941, two years before his death, Sotaesan gave the congregation his transmission verse which summarized his enlightenment experience.

The transmission verse is as follows:
"Being into nonbeing, and nonbeing into being,
Turning and turning in the ultimate,
Being and nonbeing are both empty,
Yet this emptiness is also complete."

When Sotaesan delivered his transmission verse, he said, "Although enlightened masters of the past disclosed their transmission verse on their deathbeds to only a few of their students, I am handing down this transmission verse now in advance for all people. Whether you receive the dharma or not depends entirely on your study and practice. Therefore, each of you should carry out your study and practice so that you will have no regret later."

He also explained his transmission verse with the following words, "Being is a realm of change; nonbeing is a realm of unchanging. Yet, this is a realm that cannot be called either being nor nonbeing. It is also expressed as 'turning and turning' and 'ultimate', but these are only expressions provided as a way of teaching. So, what is the point of saying 'both empty' or 'complete'? Since this realm is the true essence of our original nature, do not try to understand it through rationalizations; rather, you should awaken to this realm through contemplation."

To prepare the dharma for after his death, Sotaesan also delivered the newly designed Won Buddhist doctrinal chart and said:

"The quintessence of my teachings and dharma lies herein; however, how many of you can understand my true intention? It seems that only a few of you in this congregation today can receive it fully. This is first due to your minds being attached to wealth and sex, and secondly, your inclination toward reputation and vanity, which has prevented you from one-minded concentration. With this, you must decide what to leave behind and what to seek. You will find success only by making a big decision and taking just a single path."[2]

He also emphasized three goals of the organization: spreading the dharma, education, and charity. He said, "In the future, we must always promote these three in tandem so that our initiative may be flawless."

A year before his nirvana, Sotaesan often urged his disciples to complete the compilation of *The Principal Book of Won Buddhism*, which was in progress. He would often stay up late at night editing the work.

When the manuscript was completed, he had it sent immediately to the printers, saying to his disciples:

"Since time is short, the book may not be complete, but the essence of my whole life's aspiration and vision are basically expressed in this one volume. Therefore, please receive and keep this book so that you may learn through its words, realize with your own mind, and practice with your body. Let this dharma be transmitted forever, throughout tens of thousands of generations. In the future, people throughout the world, will recognize this dharma and be deeply impressed. Countless people will hold this dharma in reverence."[3]

2. Ibid, 402-403.
3. Ibid, 400.

Sotaesan also said:

"It is vital that you transmit my dharma to future generations by writing it down and explaining it orally. However, it is more important for you to put the dharma into practice and realize it with your minds, so this dharma lineage is never severed. If you do so, your merit will be beyond measure."[4]

His Passing

On May 16, 1943, Sotaesan presented his final dharma talk.

"On my way here to the Dharma Hall, I met several children who were playing in the woods by the side of the road. Upon seeing me, one of them signaled to the others, and together they all stood up and bowed. From their behavior, it was apparent they were maturing. When people are very young, they don't understand the nature of family relationships or their responsibilities to family members. As they mature, this becomes more apparent. Likewise, when practitioners are ignorant, they do not understand the particulars of how one becomes a buddha, bodhisattva, or ordinary sentient being, or the understanding of relationships between themselves and heaven and earth, the myriad of living things, or the pathway

---

4. Ibid, 407-408.

between birth and death. As their practice gradually evolves, they come to understand the Truth. Therefore, in the same manner that a child gradually becomes an adult, we come to understand the Way; an ordinary human being awakens and becomes a buddha and a disciple learns and becomes a master. This means that you must acquire more knowledge through learning so that you can teach the younger generations, thus become pioneers in delivering all sentient beings and curing the world of suffering. It is said in the *Yin-fu ching* (Dark Amulet Scripture), 'Birth is the root of death; death is the root of birth.' Birth and death are like the rotation of the four seasons and the recurrence of day and night. All things in the universe operate on the principle of Truth. Buddhas and bodhisattvas are not ignorant about birth and death; rather they are free from them, unlike ordinary sentient beings who are constrained by them. However, the births and deaths of the physical bodies of buddhas and bodhisattvas or ordinary sentient beings are all the same. Therefore, believe in both the persona and dharma, and work hard to gain freedom from delusion regarding birth and death, coming and going. We hold regular dharma meetings so that the participants can be of service to each other, sharing knowledge and experience to gain insight and grow. Be careful not to come and go in vain; the matter of birth and death is great and change occurs rapidly. It is not something to be taken lightly."[5]

5. Ibid, 405-407.

That Sunday morning, Sotaesan seemed well and hearty. After the dharma service, he partook in his usual lunch of steamed rice wrapped in leafy greens. However, as the afternoon progressed, he experienced chest discomfort, and his countenance turned pale and feeble. After the doctor's examination, Sotaesan was diagnosed with cerebral anemia. The doctor administered an injection of camphor to produce a stimulating effect in the chest to increase the red blood cell count. Nevertheless, his condition continued to deteriorate. His disciples implored him to go to the hospital, but he refused and insisted that he would be fine. Ten days later, on May 27th, he was taken to Iri Hospital and treated by Dr. Wakaski. The treatment was of no avail, and Sotaesan entered into nirvana. He was fifty-three years old. It was June 1, 1943, two years before Korea's liberation from Japanese rule.

Sotaesan led and taught his students selflessly for twenty-eight years after he had attained great enlightenment. When he entered nirvana, the Japanese police were relieved and said, "Sotaesan, the Gandhi of Korea has left. Now The Society of the Study of Buddhadharma will perish."

Before and after the funeral service, his disciples witnessed several miracles. His body emitted light and the smell of incense lingered. Ten days after his cremation, the Headquarters emitted a glow as if it were on fire. The light was so bright that some disciples rushed from Iri Station, which was two miles away, to put the fire out.

His disciples scheduled the public memorial to be held for

nine days. The Japanese police did not permit the ceremonies to continue as planned, and the mourning period was reduced to six days. The funeral service itself was held on June 6, 1943, six days after his passing, in the Great Enlightenment Hall. The number of attendants for the funeral procession was limited to two-hundred. Fifty-five people shouldered the bier carrying his casket to the crematorium.

During that era, it was a prevalent tradition that when a Buddhist master passed into nirvana, his disciples would seek out sari from the ashes after cremation. These crystals are regarded as sacred relics, symbolizing the achievement of profound enlightenment. While Sotaesan was alive, he would often say, "I will not leave behind any Sari. Do not try to search for anything mysterious or mystical from me. If there are such disciples who engage in this, they are not my true disciples."

As promised, Sotaesan's passing followed the natural course of human existence. This embodies the core principles of practice and human life: the Way is found in the ordinary. Such was the manner in which he both lived and departed.

The Japanese authorities closely monitored the cremation ceremony until its conclusion. They prohibited the disciples from bringing his ashes into the Headquarters. Following the 49th day of the service commemorating Sotaesan's deliverance, his ashes were placed in a public graveyard. The inscription on his tombstone bore the words, "Il-Won Master Sotaesan."

When Korea was liberated from Japan in 1945, his ashes

were moved to the Won Buddhism Headquarters. On April 25, 1949, the sacred pagoda of Sotaesan was erected to memorialize his life.

Chapter 3
Il-Won-Sang

Discovering Our True Self

A man was involved in a severe car accident when a truck unexpectedly rear-ended his vehicle. The truck totaled his car, leaving him unconscious inside. The truck driver quickly came to the rescue and pulled him safely from the wreckage. When the man regained consciousness, he immediately searched for injuries by poking around his body with his finger. To his dismay, with every touch, he felt pain. He was then transported to the hospital, where he told the doctor about his widespread discomfort.

However, after a thorough examination, the doctor told him that the only injury he incurred was to the finger he had used to check himself for injuries.

When a wagon stops, we whip the horse so the wagon will start moving again. The horse that pulls the wagon of our life is our mind. We often forget the importance of our mind because it is so fundamental in our life. If we make a disciplined effort to be mindful, we can control our mind rather than being controlled by it. With focused practice, we are more likely to arrive at the destination of freedom, happiness, and success. When our mind is not healthy, our body experiences pain and our life seems out of alignment. This is like the man who used his hurt finger to locate possible injuries, but attributed the ache he felt to his entire body.

Many young Koreans engage in volunteer work in developing countries. They often work with children who have no access to electricity or clean water and live in one room with their entire families. However, when the young Korean men and women return home, they frequently say that the children they helped seemed happier than people in Korea, and that they learned life lessons from those "poor" people. During the Industrial Revolution, many social scientists thought a utopia would eventually emerge—a place where people would no longer worry about securing enough food or clothing. Yet, many of us are still far from achieving happiness today, even if we don't have to worry about the basic necessities of life.

When cars were first invented and commercialized, people expected to have more free time and relaxation. But if we assess the reality of the current human condition, do we find that people with cars lead more harmonious lives? Does the possession of electronic devices bring relaxation? Does the internet reduce daily stress?

The World Happiness Index shows that this is not the case. In fact, depression and suicide rates are far higher in developed countries than in so-called underdeveloped countries. Many material possessions can benefit us and make our lives more convenient, productive, and materially richer. It is difficult to deny this reality. However, we need to reflect on why so many people in developed countries are unhappy. The fact is that our lives are not meant to revolve around the acquisition of material possessions.

There is a story about a rich man who lived in India. One day, while walking up a hill on his land, he tripped over a sharp rock, and fell. He was angry, so he ordered his servants to cover the entire hill with leather. Hearing this, his young daughter said, "Papa, why don't you put on leather shoes instead of covering the hill with leather?"

This story illustrates the common error of trying to impose our own ideas of happiness onto external circumstances.

The material circumstances and conditions of our lives will never be perfect. It is important to keep in mind that individual and collective conceptions of an ideal environment are inevitably subjective. According to one survey, many Korean people rate themselves as lower middle class. Yet, from the perspective of developing countries, most Koreans are considered privileged.

This does not mean our efforts to improve our external conditions are not valuable. The point is that we need to change our minds first. When we change our minds, our contexts naturally change and the perceived issues we face in our lives resolve themselves.

Sotaesan said, "The study of any science has limitations in its uses, but if we learn how to study the mind's functions, we can utilize that knowledge without interruption. Therefore, mind practice is the basis for all other studies."[1]

Many consider the study of the mind to be the most important research topic in the 21st century. Only when we can rediscover and train our original mind can we attain freedom and happiness.

One day, disciples of the Buddha debated over what was the scariest thing in the world. One disciple said that the scariest thing in the world was a venomous snake. This was because during that time, quite a number of practitioners who practiced in the forest were bitten by snakes and died. Another disciple said that anger was the scariest thing in the world. He likened anger to a fire that burns our minds and relationships. The last disciple said that love was the scariest thing. He said the desire called "love" can blind and imprison us. Obsession, a most dreadful expression of love, can be the scariest thing in the world, he said.

When they met with the Buddha and asked him the same question, the Buddha answered that the most dreadful thing is ignorance. The root cause of our suffering and distress is our ignorance about our true self, along with not knowing where we have come from and where we are.

1. *The Scriptures of Won-Buddhism*, 355.

A prophet once lamented, "My people are destroyed for lack of knowledge [of God]."

Happiness that comes from a changing environment is conditional and fragile. Therefore, it can never be everlasting and is impermanent.

The happiness or freedom that results from the realization of our original mind or true self is perpetual and indestructible.

The Buddha said that it is when, and only when, we realize our true nature, that we are free from suffering and distress. Wisdom is not simply for show, for fun or for philosophical speculation. It is really a practical necessity in order to live a life of freedom and happiness.

In Won Buddhism, our true self or original mind, is symbolized as a circle, which is called Il-Won-Sang. Il-Won-Sang means One Circle Image.

Discovering and becoming united with Il-Won-Sang or our true self is the only path to perpetual, everlasting and indestructible happiness and freedom.

Twenty-five hundred years ago, the Buddha embarked upon this journey. Why don't we invest the time to follow this same path? The greatest, most important voyage is to discover our true self and attain great enlightenment.

The Meaning of Il-Won-Sang

In Won Buddhism, Il-Won-Sang or One Circle Image is both the object of faith and the model for practice. Il-Won or One Circle represents our true nature and ultimate reality.

- Il ('一') means 'one' or 'absolute.'
- Won ('圓') means 'circle' or 'perfect and complete.'
- Sang ('相') means 'image' or 'an outward appearance.'

Il-Won or One Circle represents our true nature or our original mind, which is perfect and complete, utterly impartial and selfless.

From ancient times, many spiritual traditions have expressed the universal truth through the image of a circle. In early Christianity, God was depicted as a circle. Saint Augustine said, "God is a circle whose center is everywhere, and whose circumference is nowhere." In Zen Buddhism, Buddha nature or our original mind is also symbolized by a circular image.

In Won Buddhist temples, the Buddha statue is replaced by the Il-Won-Sang (O) image.

- O -

Il-Won is the Dharmakaya Buddha,
the origin of all things in the universe,
the truth that all buddhas and sages are enlighten to,
and the original nature of all sentient beings.

Upon returning home from school, a young boy noticed his grandmother intently searching for something. "Grandma, what are you looking for?" he inquired. "A needle," she replied. Puzzled, he asked, "Where did you lose it?" "In the living room," she answered. Perplexed, he queried, "Then why are you searching for it in the yard?" She responded, "Because the light is better out here!"[2]

Similarly, one who seeks happiness without understanding their true self or Il-Won is like the grandmother searching for the needle in the wrong place.

Sotaesan said:

"The reason that practitioners seek to awaken to profound truth is to apply that truth in their everyday lives. Whenever we encounter the Il-Won-Sang, we should take it as a koan or spiritual question to contemplate, so that we can see our true nature and attain enlightenment. Additionally, we can use Il-Won Sang as a model in order to keep practicing skillfully in

---

2. Dosung Yoo, *Thunderous Silence*. 2.

our daily lives. Those of you who understand this truth will venerate Il-Won-Sang each time you encounter it; as if it were a portrait of your parents."[3]

In a village in Korea, a traveling silk merchant stopped to rest beneath a tree. Upon waking, he was aghast to find his precious silk rolls missing. Desperate, he hastened to the governor's office to report the theft and plead for the thief's capture. When the governor asked if there had been any witnesses, the merchant could only mention a nearby wooden totem pole. The governor, with a grave expression, solemnly declared, "Then we must question the totem pole, as it is the sole witness." He commanded his men to fetch the totem pole and set a court hearing.

Word of the governor's eccentric decision spread quickly. On the day of the trial, the village courtroom brimmed with intrigued locals. With gravity, the governor had the totem pole presented and bound in ropes. He boomed a question at it, asking if it had seen the theft. Met with silence, he grew more forceful, demanding an answer. His feigned fury peaked as he ordered the totem pole to be chained and beaten, shouting louder with each blow. The spectacle drew laughter from the audience, and the governor, feigning further outrage, commanded all who laughed to produce three rolls of silk within a week.

As the week concluded, many villagers brought forth silk rolls. The governor had the merchant identify his property, and

3. *The Scripture of Wonbulkyo*. 115-116.

then questioned the silk-bringing villagers about their seller. Their answers pointed to a single individual: the thief. In a move that seemed unorthodox, the governor had ingeniously uncovered the perpetrator.[4]

Just as the governor's unorthodox methods led to the truth, contemplation or meditation on the Il-Won-Sang as a spiritual query guides us toward enlightenment. This deeper realization enhances the freedom we experience in every moment, regardless of our external circumstances.

---

4. Kyongbong, *Touch the Door Latch In the Middle of the Night*, 15–17.

Il-Won and Il-Won-Sang

Il-Won (一圓)

When a baby is born, he or she is given a name composed by parents or other family members. 'Il-Won' is the name for universal truth or ultimate reality, composed by Sotaesan after he attained great enlightenment in 1924 at the age of twenty-six.

In traditional Buddhism, our true nature or ultimate reality is called Dharmakaya Buddha. In Taoism, the ultimate reality is called the Way (道), Tao, or Nature; in the Judeo-Christian tradition, God, or Allah, and in Confucianism, 'the ultimate (無極)' or 'grand ultimate (太極).'

A person can be a child to their parents, a sibling to a brother or sister, a teacher to their students, and a student to their teachers. Names differ according to one's position. However, the person is the same regardless of their name or position; the original essence of one's true self always remains the same.

When buddhas or bodhisattvas came to this world, they each

assigned a different name to their understanding of the truth. Their approach or emphasis varied, depending on the historic period and location in which the sages lived and taught, and the level of people's intelligence and spirituality. To guide people toward awakening, they utilized different perspectives and approaches. That is why the one ultimate reality has many names.

Sotaesan said:

"In the past, religious founders appeared in response to the needs of that time, so they could provide all sentient beings with proper guidance on how to conduct their lives. However, the core principles and delivery of their teachings differed because of their location and the time period in which they lived. This is comparable to there being different areas of specialty in medical science. Buddhism, for example, took the formlessness of all things as its core principle and taught the truth that is free from arising and ceasing, as well as the principle of retribution and response of cause and effect, thus illuminating the path where ignorance is transformed into awakening. Confucianism took the form of all things in the universe as its core principle and taught the three duties, five relationships, and the four constants of benevolence: righteousness, propriety, and knowledge. Thereby, it mainly elucidates the path whereby one cultivates oneself, regulates one's family, governs one's country, and realizes peace in the world. Daoism took the Way of the natural universe as its core principle and taught techniques for nourishing original nature, principally elucidating the path of tranquility and nonaction. Although these three paths have core principles that differ from one another, they all have the common goal of remedying the world and benefiting all living beings. In the past, however, these three teachings of Buddhism, Confucianism, and Daoism have mainly disseminated their own doctrines. But in the future, it will not be enough to deliver the whole world through partial subjects alone. Hence, we have integrated all of these doctrines, unifying the teachings of Cultivation, Inquiry, and Choice into the Il-Won (One Circle), as well as on the wholeness of both spirit and flesh and the simultaneous practice of universal principles and human affairs. Anyone who practices these methods of study will not only become well versed in the fundamental teachings of these three religions but will also be able to accept the teachings of all religions, and all dharmas will return to the one mind, attaining enlightenment to the great Way that reaches everywhere."[5]

Il-Won-Sang (一圓相)

Il-Won-Sang is the symbol of truth offered by Sotaesan. He expressed the shape of truth as a circle. Thus, for Won Buddhism, Il-Won-Sang as the doctrine becomes both the object of faith and the model of practice. Therefore, Il-Won-Sang is the shape of

---

5. *The Scripture of Wonbulkyo*, 111.

truth, and part of truth, but not the entirety of it.

Sotaesan elucidated that while the buddha image manifests the physical form of the buddha, Il-Won-Sang manifests the mind-essence of the Buddha. He added that the physical form represents the human form, but the mind-essence is the original essence of truth. He clearly stated that the image of Il-Won-Sang is the symbol of the original essence of truth.

Therefore, the circular image is only a model for teaching the true Il-Won. It is like pointing at the moon with your finger: your finger is not the real moon.

Master Chongsan, the Second Head Dharma Master who succeeded Sotaesan, explained Il-Won-Sang as below:

> "If you are only given the name of someone you do not know, it is difficult to gain an understanding of who they are. But if you are shown a photograph, you will have a way to identify them. Similarly, because Sotaesan has shown us a picture of the Truth through the Il-Won-Sang, it is much easier to grasp the meaning. The Il-Won-Sang is the image of truth in its totality. If one takes this image of truth as the object of inquiry and continues to practice devotedly, then one will be able to easily understand the realm of truth."[6]

Regarding the relationship between Il-Won and Il-Won-Sang,

---

6. Ibid, 820-821.

Sotaesan said:

"That circular image is a model for teaching the true Il-Won. It is like pointing at the moon with your finger: your finger is not the real moon. In the same way, a practitioner must discover the true Il-Won through the model of Il-Won-Sang, guard Il-Won's true nature and practice embodying Il-Won's perfect and single point-ed mind. Then, the truth of Il-Won-Sang and our lives will perfectly align."[7]

One of his disciples asked, "What is the difference between worshiping the buddha image and worshiping Il-Won-Sang?" Sotaesan answered, "Worshiping the buddha image has meaning only for the descendant disciples' commemoration of and reverence for the Buddha's character. But the meaning of worshiping Il-Won-Sang is indeed wide and profound. Rather than revering the Buddha's character alone as the object of faith, we revere and have faith in all things in the universe as if they were the buddha and seek in them the origins of our transgressions and merits, suffering and happiness. Also, we take Il-Won-Sang as the model for our practice and aim to develop a character that is as perfect as Il-Won-Sang. This is the general difference."[8]

---

[7]. Ibid, 114.
[8]. Ibid, 118.

Faith in Il-Won-Sang

The Meaning of Faith in Won Buddhism

Venerable Daesan, the Third Head Dharma Master of Won Buddhism, said, "There have been two significant discoveries that have benefited all humans. One is Buddha's discovery of our mind-nature, and the other is Master Sotaesan's discovery of Grace. There is a reason we have two eyes. One is for looking inward and observing our mind and the other is for looking outward and finding Grace."

The term Grace in Won Buddhism signifies the interdependency and interconnection between all things. Regarding human existence, all things in the universe are classified into four groups, known as the Fourfold Grace: the Grace of Heaven and Earth, the Grace of Parents, the Grace of Fellow Beings, and the Grace of Laws.

The Fourfold Grace is the manifestation of Dharmakaya (Truth) Buddha or Il-Won-Sang. One could say that the Fourfold Grace and Dharmakaya Buddha are two sides of the same coin. In Won Buddhism, we see the world from the perspective of

Grace, which implies "co-existence," "interdependence" and "oneness."

The Fourfold Grace is the source of all blessings, and blessings come from being aware of and requiting the Fourfold Grace.

The Method of Faith in Won Buddhism

Treating every living thing as Buddha is an act of faith in Won Buddhism and is expressed in the motto: "Everywhere a Buddha Image, Every Act a Buddha Offering."

> Kwangjon asked again, "How do we practice faith in Il-Won-Sang?" Sotaesan replied, "Take Il-Won-Sang as the object of faith, and believing in its truth, pursue merit and happiness. If we were to specify the contents of Il-Won-Sang, it is, in fact, the Fourfold Grace. If we were to specify the contents of the Fourfold Grace, it is, in fact, all things in the universe. There is nothing among the myriad things in heaven and earth or the dharma realm of empty space that is not the buddha. Thus, regardless of time or place, we must never ne-glect to maintain a respectful state of mind and should treat the world's myriad things with the same pure mind and pious attitude we have towards the venerable Buddha. We should also exert ourselves to make bud-dha offerings directly to the myriad things themselves, thus creating merit and happiness in a practical manner. In sum, we are prompting people to transform a

partial faith into a well-rounded faith and a superstitious faith into a realistic faith."[9]

In Won Buddhism, there are two ways of making offerings to the buddha. One is a buddha offering to the Truth. This offering is through the formless void of the dharma world. The other is a practical buddha offering. This is a buddha offering to the Fourfold Grace, i.e. to all beings in the universe.

Realistic faith and practical buddha offerings characterize faith in Il-Won Sang.

Once, while Sotaesan was living at Pongnae hermitage, an old couple was passing by and commented that their daughter-in-law was so ill-tempered and disrespectful that they were on their way to Silsang monastery to make a buddha offering so they could turn her into a good-natured daughter-in-law. Upon hearing their problem, Sotaesan said to them, "How do you know to make a buddha offering to the Buddha image but not to the living buddha?" The old couple asked, "Where is the living buddha?" The Founding Master replied, "The daughter-in-law who lives in your home is the living buddha, since she is the one with the capacity to offer you filial piety or disrespect. Why don't you try making an offering to her first?" They asked, "How should we make such an offering?" Sotaesan

---

9. Ibid, 113.

answered, "With the money you were going to use for the buddha offering, buy her a gift she would appreciate and treat her with the same respect you would the Buddha. Then, depending on how sincere you are, the effect of your buddha offering will appear." When the couple returned home, they did as they were told and within a few months; she became a devoted daughter-in-law. The old couple returned to Sotaesan and thanked him repeatedly. Sotaesan said to his disciples sitting beside him, "This is a practical buddha offering that directly targets the specific object of transgression and merit."[10]

Treating others as buddhas or helping others in various ways is a great way to create blessings. According to the Buddha's words, blessing and merits are important assets for practitioners to attain great enlightenment. Without many blessings, it may be difficult to find an ideal environment that supports our practice or allows us meet a good teacher or dharma friend. Ultimately, blessings and wisdom will eventually lead practitioners to great enlightenment.

The Purpose of Faith

The purpose of faith is to receive and enjoy blessings and merits. Blessings and merits originate from the Fourfold Grace, the

10. Ibid, 120-121.

manifestation of Dharmakaya Buddha, or Il-Won-Sang.

Sotaesan emphasized the importance of having realistic faith, as opposed to superstitious faith. Blessings or merits arise when we express gratitude and requite the Fourfold Grace: the Grace of Heaven and Earth, the Grace of Parents, the Grace of Fellow Beings, and the Grace of Laws.

Sotaesan specifically addressed our indebtedness to the Fourfold Grace, highlighting the foundational role these graces play in our lives.

The Essence of Indebtedness to Heaven and Earth

1. Because of the air in the sky, we are able to live by inhaling and exhaling.
2. Because of the support of the ground, we are able to live on the Earth.
3. Because of the radiance of the sun and moon, we come to distinguish and know the innumerable phenomena in the universe.
4. Because of the grace of wind, clouds, rain, and dew, we come to live off the products created.
5. As heaven and earth neither arise nor cease, immeasurable beings come to attain endless life in accordance with the Way.

The Essence of Indebtedness to Parents

1. Thanks to our parents, we receive this body, which is the foundation of all human affairs and universal principles.
2. Parents or Guardians do their best to raise and protect us, until we gain self-power.
3. Through their right or wrong words and actions, they teach us human functions and responsibilities, and guide us into human society.

The Essence of Indebtedness to Fellow Beings

1. Scholars study and research to direct and educate the public in various ways.
2. Farmers plant and raise crops to provide materials for our clothing and food.
3. Artisans manufacture all types of goods to provide us with shelter and necessities.
4. Merchants trade various material goods to help make our lives convenient.
5. Even birds and beasts, the trees and grass are essential to humanity.

The Essence of Indebtedness to Laws

1. Sages come to the world according to the times, and by means of religions and morality they teach human beings to

follow the right path.

2. Laws enable us to protect lives and foster knowledge. They also grant us the ability to establish institutions for scholars, farmers, artisans, and merchants, and apply ourselves in edification and admonition to the law.

3. Laws enable us to live peacefully by reproving injustice and promoting justice through distinguishing right and wrong, benefit and harm, and by thus maintaining tranquility and order.[11]

Knowing the Graces is not enough. To embody Grace and not cause suffering in our lives, we must express and requite gratitude to the Fourfold Grace.

Showing gratitude and requiting the Fourfold Grace is the way to live a blessed and abundant life. Requiting Grace allows us to receive blessings and merits for ourselves as well as for others.

---

11. Ibid, 28-37.

The Need for Spiritual Cultivation

A few years ago in Seoul, a high school girl jumped off a seven-story apartment building. In her room she left a school report card and a suicide note that said, "This must be good enough for you."

Just like many other students in Korea, she studied hard and was under a lot of pressure because of schoolwork. She always got the second highest grades in her class. But her mother always pushed her to be the best, saying that she was doing it for her daughter's sake. However, despite her mother's wish, the daughter could not surpass one student, no matter how hard she tried. One day, the top student did not do well on an exam because she was feeling ill. Finally, the girl who had always been second best, briefly became the best in her class. However, on the same day she received her grade on the exam, she ended her life.

Why did she make such a choice? Her suicide may perhaps reflect the anxiety many students (and even many adults) feel as they struggle to survive and succeed in an overwhelmingly competitive society.

Should we condemn her mother and say she was a bad parent? I believe she must have loved her daughter dearly. Most likely, she was just like many parents whose words and thoughts reflect the life of a person who has accepted the inevitable extreme competitiveness of our capitalistic.

In a success-oriented culture, people must constantly use their minds to succeed.

For most people, technological and scientific developments have created the habit of being constantly engaged in mental activity and stimulation, with less and less involvement in physical work. It seems that to survive in the present world, perpetual thinking is required.

These mental habits, along with the anxieties of modern life may become overwhelming when we try to practice sitting meditation. Our minds are immediately bombarded with delusions, wandering thoughts, worries, and many stimuli.

Even when we rest, we cannot stop using our minds. We try to refresh our minds by watching TV, surfing the web, or talking on the cell phone. We often feel there is a need to snack between meals, not because we are hungry, but because our minds are accustomed to constant stimulation. We get bored quickly if we are not engaged in sensory experiences.

I revisited Seoul last year after being away for a long time. I was shocked to see that almost everyone on the subway—kids, students, and adults—was focused on looking at their cell phones during the entire ride. This is a very common scene in western countries as well.

Both our muscles and our mental powers get stronger as we exercise them. But they also need time to rest and recuperate. A battery gradually loses power and will not function if we use it without recharging. People who have exhausted their mental power are more susceptible to external stimuli and stress, and can be more easily swayed by the influence of others. We need our mental capacity in order to see, listen, speak or think. We also need to recharge our mental energy when it is drained by such activities. However, in today's rapidly advancing world, we seldom have time to fully recharge our mental energy. This is because we constantly use up our mental energy when we speak, work, watch TV/movies, use computers, or play games on our cellphones. We expend our mental energy even when we think we are resting, because we really don't stop thinking and the mind remains engaged.

However, we can strengthen our mental power in various ways. One way is to give our minds a break every morning and during the evening through exercise and meditation.

Buddha called the mind bombarded by incessant thoughts, worries, information, and stimulation, "a burning mind."

Buddha said, "Monks and nuns, this world is burning! With what is it burning? How is it burning? The eyes are burning, the ears are burning, and the mind is burning. With what fires are they burning? With the fire of greed, anger, and hatred and with the fire of ignorance and delusion. By ending your grasping and delusion and not clinging to your eyes, ears, and mind, you can find freedom."

Sotaesan instructed us to rest our mind and recharge our spirit by reciting the buddha's name and practicing seated meditation. There are many ways to rejuvenate a mind that has been drained by constant use. We can extinguish the fire in our mind by chanting or sitting meditation.

Here is a list of some of the benefits derived from reciting the buddha's name and sitting meditation. These are listed in *The Principal Book of Won Buddhism*.

1. Rash and thoughtless behavior will decrease and gradually disappear.
2. The six sense organs and their functions will become balanced.
3. Suffering from illnesses will diminish, and your face will naturally shine.
4. Your memory will improve.
5. You will become more patient.
6. Your attachments will lessen.
7. Unhealthy states of mind will transform into righteous states of mind.
8. The innate wisdom of your original nature will radiate.
9. You will begin to enjoy a state of ultimate bliss.

10. You will gain freedom from the cycle of birth and death.[12]

We do not live to practice; we practice to live. When we cultivate and strengthen our mind and spirit, we become less easily influenced and tossed about by external challenges and the world's temptations. Instead, our lives become far more peaceful and content.

There was a cowboy riding his horse alongside his Native American friend. Suddenly, he realized his friend and the horse were no longer beside him. Perplexed, he turned his horse around, and rode back until he found the Native American man who had gotten off his horse and was standing still. The cowboy asked him what he was doing. His friend answered, "I was riding my horse when suddenly I felt that only my body was on the horse and that my mind had wandered somewhere else. So, I realized I had to retrace the path back to where my mind had departed. Now, having done that, I am standing here for a moment regathering my mind, so I can consciously resume my path."

In fact, many of us are mindlessly driving the car called "life." Many of us just try to outrun the cars next to us, not knowing where we are going. The faster we drive, the less we observe on the way. Like the mindful Native American man, if we want to

---

12. Ibid, 66.

know whether we are going in the right direction, we need to slow down—or ideally, stop the car, get out, look around, and maybe even retrace some of our steps.

Practice of Il-Won-Sang

The Meaning of Practice

Spiritual practice means training our mind to be able to realize universal truth and restore our original nature. Such practice eventually leads us to attain freedom of mind: the liberation of suffering and its causes. The practice of Il-Won-Sang is the practice of making a conscious and continuous effort to unify with our original mind.

When Sotaesan attained great enlightenment on April 28, 1926, the first year of Won Buddhism, he said, "All beings are of a single nature. All dharmas originate from one source. The Truth of neither arising nor ceasing, and the karmic principle of cause and effect, interact in perfect, rounded, and complete oneness."[13]

The truth of Il-Won-Sang is comprised of two principles. One is eternal life: the unchanging aspect of universal truth. The other is the karmic principle of cause and effect: the ever-changing aspect

---

13. Ibid, 95.

of universal truth. All things in the universe including all human affairs, are continuously transforming according to the principle of yin and yang. These two principles do not transcend the mind. Rather, as Buddha said, all things are created by the mind.

Sotaesan emphasized that the practice of Il-Won-Sang is to realize, nurture, and use our original mind, which is perfect and complete, utterly impartial and selfless like Il-Won-Sang.

In *The Principal Book of Won Buddhism*, the practice of Il-Won-Sang is defined as follows:

"Believing in and, at the same time, modeling ourselves on the truth of Il-Won-Sang, our aim is that we should know our minds, which are perfect and complete, utterly impartial and selfless like Il-Won-Sang; that we should nurture our minds, which are perfect and complete, utterly impartial and selfless like Il-Won-Sang; and that we should use our minds, which are perfect and complete, utterly impartial and selfless like Il-Won-Sang: this is the practice of Il-Won-Sang."[14]

Although our mind is originally perfect and complete, utterly impartial and selfless, we can become disturbed and deluded when we encounter difficult situations. We are then subject to engaging in wrong-doing, and lose our center or true nature. In these situations, we need to recover and maintain our original

---

14. *The Scriptures of Won-Buddhism*, 6.

mind as quickly as possible. This is achieved through the practice of Il-Won-Sang.

The Method of Practice

In our daily life, it is not easy to maintain our true nature or to maintain a well-rounded disposition, as the Buddha did.

It is necessary to know the right method to restore our true nature. Spiritual practice begins when we realize our true nature. However, realizing our true nature alone does not lead us directly to attaining Buddhahood and freedom of mind. Following our realization, we need to cultivate and nurture our mind. More importantly, we need to use our mind well in daily life. For our spiritual practice to be fruitful, our knowledge and actions must be aligned.

> The Great Master, accompanied by two disciples, Cho Song-Kwang and Chun Eum-Kwang, went for a walk in Namchoong-ni, a suburb of Iri City. Cho Song-Kwang, seeing several beautiful pine trees on the roadside, said, "Oh, such beautiful trees! I wish I could transfer them to our temple." The Great Master, hearing his words, said, "You still are not able to transcend your limited thought and narrow viewpoint. The temple never stands apart from the tree and the tree does not stand apart from our temple. Both are within our fence. What should we transfer them for? You still have the

conception of discrimination and have not found the great home of the universe." Cho asked, "What is the great home like?" The Great Master continued, "It is before you at present, but as you are unable to recognize it, I will draw its symbol for you:" Then he drew a circle, Il-Won-Sang, on the ground, and continued his talk, "This is the home of the universe, in which infinitely mysterious principles, immeasurable treasures, and infinite capabilities are stored." Chun Eum-Kwang asked, "How can we get into the home, and how can we be the master of it?" The Great Master replied, "You must obtain the key, the Three Great Powers, to gain entrance to it. The key is made of Faith, Courage, Questioning and Sincerity."[15]

The practice method to be one with our true nature, Il-Won-Sang, is three-pronged: Cultivating the Spirit, Cultivation of Wisdom, and Choice in Action.

Cultivating the Spirit means to calm the mind in order to maintain a peaceful, focused state. Cultivating Wisdom means to hone our innate wisdom and obtain knowledge of human affairs and universal principles. Choice in Action is properly using our six sense organs—eye, ear, nose, tongue, body, and mind—to make right choices throughout our daily life.

The essentials of Threefold Practice are explained in *The Principal Book of Won Buddhism*:

---

15. *The Scripture of Won Buddhism*, 274-275.

A. The Essential Purport of Cultivating the Spirit

"Spirit" (*Chongsin*) means that state in which the mind, being clear and round, calm and tranquil, is free from a tendency toward discrimination and a penchant toward attachment. "Cultivating" (*suyang*) means nourishing the spirit which is clear and round, calm and tranquil, by internally letting go of a tendency toward discrimination and a penchant toward attachment and externally not being enticed by distracting sensory conditions.

B. The Objective of Cultivating the Spirit

Sentient creatures instinctually have a natural ability to know and a desire to do certain things. Humans, the most intelligent of beings, tend to know through their ability to see, hear, and learn. Humans also have a desire to act on certain things that is exponentially greater than that of other mammals. So, if a human idly decides to seek their own satisfaction through their actions, without regard to the potential suffering that could be created, they will, in consequence, create disharmony for themselves and for those whom they love. Therefore, our aim is to engage in spiritual cultivation that strengthens the power of our mind, by removing this desire so we may attain a sound spirit.

C. The Consequences of Cultivating the Spirit

If we continue for a long time with the work of Cultivating the Spirit, our spirit will become as solid as iron or stone, and in applying ourselves to the myriad sensory conditions, autonomous power will arise in the mind, and ultimately, we will gain the power of Cultivation.

A. The Essential Purport of Inquiry into Human Affairs and Universal Principles

"Human affairs" (*sa*) means the right and wrong, benefit and harm, among human beings. "Universal principles" (*ri*) means the great and small, being and nonbeing, of heavenly creation. "Great" means the original essence of all things in the universe. "Small" means that the myriad phenomena are distinguished by their shapes and forms. "Being and nonbeing" means the cycle of nature's four seasons of spring, summer, fall, and winter, as well as wind, clouds, rain, dew, frost, and snow; the birth, aging, sickness, and death of all things; and the transformation of creation and destruction, nourishing and decay. "Inquiry" (*yongu*) means studying and mastering human affairs and universal principles.

B. The Objective of Inquiry into Human Affairs and Universal Principles

This world is constructed through the principles of great and small, being and nonbeing, and is driven by the affairs of right and wrong, benefit and harm. Therefore, as the world is vast, there are infinite types of principles; just as there are many people, there are limitless types of human affairs. However, the suffering and happiness that might inadvertently occur and the suffering and happiness that we create for ourselves are the consequences of our own making through the operation of the six sense organs. If we act whenever we please and stop whenever we please, ignorant of the right and wrong, benefit and harm, of our actions, then the activities of our six sense organs at every instant will turn into transgressions and suffering, so that our future will become a boundless sea of suffering.

C. The Consequences of Inquiry into Human Affairs and Universal Principles

If we continue with the work of Inquiry into Human Affairs and Universal Principles, we will eventually generate wisdom that remains unobstructed when examining and discerning the myriad of human affairs and universal principles, and ultimately will gain the power of Inquiry.

A. The Essential Purport of Choice in Action

"Action" (*chagŏp*) means the functioning of the six sense organs of eye, ear, nose, tongue, body, and mind in whatever one does. "Choice" (*ch'wisa*) means choosing what is right and forsaking what is wrong.

B. The Objective of Choice in Action

Even if we have gained the power that comes from Cultivating the Spirit and the power of Inquiry that comes from Inquiry into Human Affairs and Universal Principles, they will be useless if we do not put them into practice in our daily life. This would be like a tree that has a good trunk, branches, flowers, and leaves, but bears no fruit.

As a rule, why is it that as human beings we often do not choose what is right, even while knowing the right choice? Likewise, why do we not put an end to choosing what is wrong even while knowing it is wrong, so that we forsake our true nature and fall into the perilous sea of suffering? This is because we lack awareness of the practical application of right or wrong in actual situations, or even though we know what is right or wrong, we cannot control our desires, or resist falling into habitual tendencies. Therefore, our aim is to work at putting into practice the right choice at all costs and forsaking what is wrong at all costs, so that we may avoid the odious sea of suffering and welcome the yearned-for paradise.

C. The Consequences of Choice in Action

If we continue for a long time with the work of Choice in Action, we will gain the power of putting into practice the valiant choice of the right and the valiant forsaking of the wrong in applying ourselves in any situation, and ultimately will gain the power of Choice.[16]

After Sotaesan attained great enlightenment, he suffered from bouts of coughing during the winter months. This condition became especially difficult when he delivered dharma talks. Regarding this, he expressed the following to his disciples.

The Great Master developed a cough every winter, and it often interrupted his teaching. He said to the assembly, "As you know, the place of my birth, Kilyong-ni, is a place beset by unusual poverty and ignorance due to a lack of education. Fortunately, because of habits in my past lives, I had sincere spiritual aspirations since my youth and have diligently sought the Way. Unfortunately, I had no opportunity to ask questions or receive guidance. Therefore I suffered from various difficult ascetic practices. Sometimes, I would go into the mountains and stay there overnight or spend the whole day sitting in meditation on the road until dusk. I would in other instances bathe in icy water, or fast, or stay in a room that was extremely cold until I finally lost consciousness. As a result of my extreme effort, all my doubts were resolved, but a physical illness took

---

16. *The Scriptures of Won-Buddhism*, 30-36.

root in my body. Now my illness has grown increasingly worse. Because I did not know the road, there was nothing I could do at that time. Fortunately, even without performing difficult ascetic practices, you have directly learned the well-rounded dharma of Mahayana practice by benefiting from my experience. This is a great blessing for you. Generally speaking, the practice of timeless meditation and placeless meditation is the quickest way to Mahayana practice. If you practice in this manner, you will get twice the results with half the work. And you will succeed without becoming ill. I beseech you all not to fall into the error of harming your body by recognizing the uselessness of the ascetic practices that I performed before I found the path.[17]

In order to carry out the Threefold Practice skillfully and efficiently, Sotaesan suggested eleven subjects of mind practice.

Reciting the Buddha's name and Sitting Meditation are for Cultivating the Spirit.
Studying scripture, lecturing, dharma conversation, contemplating koans, learning the principle of our true nature, and keeping a mindfulness journal are for the Cultivation of Wisdom.
Keeping a Daily Mind Diary, Heedfulness, and Deportment are for Choice in Action.

17. *The Scripture of Wonbulkyo*, 170-171.

Although there are eleven subjects of training to carry out the Threefold Practice, the intended result is to eventually develop the practice of 'Timeless and Placeless Meditation.' This is the primary practice of Won Buddhism: develop the ability to maintain one-pointedness of mind anytime and in any situation. Simply stated, this teaches us how to maintain mindfulness so we can make choices based on sound thought in our daily lives.

The way to apply these eleven subjects for Threefold Practice is expressed in the Essential Dharmas of Daily Practice, which comprise a guide for practice in our daily life. It is composed of nine articles.

Essential Dharmas of Daily Practice

1. The mind is originally free from disturbance, but disturbances arise in response to sensory conditions; let us restore the equanimity of our true nature by letting go of those disturbances.
2. The mind is originally free from delusion, but delusions arise in response to sensory conditions; let us restore the wisdom of our true nature by letting go of those delusions.
3. The mind is originally free from wrong-doing, but wrong-doings arise in response to sensory conditions; let us restore the precepts of our true nature by letting go of those wrong-doings.
4. Let us replace disbelief, greed, laziness, and ignorance with belief, zeal, questioning, and dedication.

5. Let us turn a life of resentment into a life of gratitude.
6. Let us turn a life of dependency into a life of self-reliance.
7. Let us turn reluctance to learn into willingness to learn well.
8. Let us turn reluctance to teach into willingness to teach well.
9. Let us turn a self-serving mind into eagerness to serve the good of all.[18]

Sotaesan added, "If you do so, there is no one who cannot become a buddha."

"The purpose of having you recite the Essential Dharmas of Daily Practice in the morning and evening does not lie in simply reciting the words. Rather, it is intended to help you grasp their meaning in your hearts and assess it in your minds, reviewing them generally once a day, and, more specifically, examining them each time you are faced with sensory conditions."[19]

Why Should We Practice?

The reason why we should carry out mind practice is simple. The body is driven by the mind. When our mind is not empowered, it does not contain sufficient wisdom regarding human affairs

---

18. Ibid, 54.
19. *The Scriptures of Won-Buddhism*, 141.

and universal principles. Consequently, we will tend to create transgressions, and this will lead us to suffering. In order to live a happy and free life, we need to discipline our mind.

There is a saying: People hate suffering but love its cause.

The Buddha said that as long as the wisdom of people's original mind is tainted by the three mental poisons of greed, hatred and delusion, the mind will not be free from ignorance. This ignorance is the origin of all our transgressive actions, which directly causes our suffering.

The Founding Master continued, "The Buddha's unsurpassed, great path is immensely high, deep, and vast; hence, his wisdom and capacity cannot be expressed verbally or in writing. However, the following points generally express the penetrating power of the Buddha's wisdom. While ordinary people are aware that birth and death exists, but are ignorant of eternal life, the Buddha knew the principle that is free from birth and death and the existence of endless lifetimes through the process of rebirth. We do not even understand the fundamental principle governing our own being, but the Buddha understood the fundamental principle governing all things in the universe. We fall into unwholesome destinies because we cannot clearly distinguish between choices that will lead us down a good path and those that will not. However, after delivering himself, the Buddha gained the ability to deliver all sentient beings from unwholesome to wholesome destinies.

While we do not understand how we create suffering and happiness for ourselves, nor the suffering and happiness that inadvertently befalls all sentient beings, the Buddha clearly knew why these occur. We enjoy the fruits of our merit but can do nothing when it is exhausted, but the Buddha had the ability to restore merit once it had been depleted. We live without realizing how dull or bright our wisdom is becoming, but the Buddha had the ability to brighten wisdom that had dulled and sustain wisdom once it was attained. Under the influence of our own greed, hatred, and delusion, we commit wrongful acts, but the Buddha was never influenced by, and therefore never acted on greed, hatred, and delusion. We are attached to the existence of all things in the universe but are ignorant of the realm where all things are non-existent. However, the Buddha realized the empty nature of reality, where existence resides amid non-existence and non-existence amid existence. We have no knowledge of the six destinies, referred to as heavenly beings, human beings, asuras, animals, hungry ghosts, and the denizens of hell. Nor do we know the four types of birth—viviparous, oviparous, moisture-born, and metamorphic, but the Buddha even knew the principle governing rebirth between the six destinies and the four types of birth. We often harm others for our own benefit, but the Buddha, when dealing with any matter, sought to create mutual benefit. Yet, when that became impossible, he found blessings and joy in benefiting others, regardless of his own gain or loss. Even if it meant risking his own life. While we only view our possessions as the ones that belong to us, the Buddha saw all things in the universe as his possessions. For us, our home is only the house in which we live, and our family only those we are related to, but for the Buddha, all worlds in the ten-directions were his home, and all sentient beings his family. Hence, our aim is to strive to attain the Buddha's wisdom and abilities and exert ourselves to deliver all sentient beings."[20]

When we read and contemplate this passage, we realize that practitioners must model themselves after this great wisdom. This requires training our minds, which is not an easy task. Yet, for the benefit of our lives and that of others, we need to cultivate and recover our true nature. The challenge of mind practice is that not many people make the necessary effort to realize this truth and put it into action.

The following verse may be helpful.

In 1919, after the levee project was completed, the members said, "When we first began, this project seemed almost as difficult as constructing a high mountain on flat land. However, now that our task is complete, building a levee seems rather easy. Yet, how difficult it will be to attain the Way!" Overhearing this, Sotaesan said, "You speak this way because you do not yet know how to attain the Way. However, once you know it,

---

20. Ibid, 308-310.

it will be easier than eating a meal. How can attaining a content and present state of mind be as difficult as constructing a levee? If you are unable to understand my meaning, keep in mind what I have said and think about it again after you have awakened to the way of practice.[21]

There is one thing we need to understand: Even the light of the wisdom of enlightened teachers can be darkened if they do not continue to practice.

The following story expresses this clearly.
After completing the embankment project, Sotaesan went to Wolmyeong Hermitage in Byeonsan. There he found a couple of verses on a wooden pillar that said, 'What is the thing that is not associated with all dharmas?'
At first, he could not understand the meaning. He realized that he had excessively expended his mind and energy while he devoted himself wholeheartedly to the embankment project, and had neglected to have enough time for his own spiritual cultivation. That is why he could not quickly grasp the meaning of that koan.

Even after one attains enlightenment, one should continue to do *Borim* (保任) or follow-up practice, which is a practice after awakening.

---

21. *The Scripture of Wonbulkyo*, 100.

When this happened, Sotaesan took three days to rest. He was then able to realize the meaning of the koan since his level of spirituality and wisdom was restored.

Taking this truth deeply into our own hearts and minds, let us all exert ourselves to practice continuously.

Obstacles to Practice

When we embark on the long journey of spiritual practice, we will encounter various obstacles. Several obstacles occur frequently and can become serious hindrances to practitioners.

These challenges result from one-sided practice and a hasty mind. The pitfalls that practitioners of an intermediate capacity encounter include false spiritual openings and enjoying supernatural occurrences.

One-sided or biased practice refers to a practitioner tending to concentrate only on the practice they enjoy while disregarding the importance of maintaining a well-balanced Threefold Practice.

A hasty mind refers to a practitioner being over-eager and rushing to accomplish their goal.

Practitioners with intermediate level spirituality tend to encounter the following pitfall:

The Founding Master said, "The spiritual capacities of all practitioners vary by thousands and tens of thousands of degrees, but they may generally be categorized into the three levels of high, medium, and low. High spiritual capacity refers to that capacity in which judgment and belief are immediately established upon seeing and hearing the right dharma, so that one carries out all spiritual practices with self-confidence. Medium spiritual capacity refers to that capacity in which one neither comprehends with precision nor is totally ignorant, and so, being unable to resolve one's doubts, is always weighing the dharma and one's teacher. Low spiritual capacity refers to that capacity in which one is unable to differentiate the perverse from the upright, and so, if well guided, conforms directly to that guidance without calculating or doubting. Of these three spiritual capacities, high is most valued and desired in religious orders. A person of high spiritual capacity will have no delays in his or her practice and will contribute greatly to the expansion of the order. The capacity that is second most worthwhile to guide is a person of low spiritual capacity who has a sincerely believing mind; for, although they may not have self-confidence, their dedicated effort to progress will not cease since they value the dharma and sincerely believe in the teacher. Thus, they will ultimately be able to succeed. The one who is most difficult to guide and the most fickle, however, is a person of medium capacity. Such a person is likely to take the dharma lightly and to look down on the teacher. In all matters such a person lacks genuine sincerity, so it is extremely difficult for him or her to experience success in their practice or in their work. Therefore, those at the medium level must work hard to transcend that level. Of those at the low level, some may jump straight to the high level; but for those who cannot and who instead advance by passing through the stage of medium capacity, that is a dangerous phase that they must be cautious about."[22]

Heoryung or false spiritual opening sometimes occurs when a practitioner's mind is calm and focused as the result of meditation practice or other forms of spiritual cultivation. Practitioners then have the ability to spontaneously predict others' futures or read their minds. Some people then believe that a person who possesses this capability is an awakened one, but this is the result of the practice of spiritual cultivation and has nothing to do with awakening.

Performing miracles or supernatural abilities, like walking on water or into fire, seeing others' past lives, or summoning winds and rains, can occur on the journey of spiritual practice. We should clearly understand that enlightenment is realizing our true nature and understanding the ultimate reality, and it has nothing to do with possessing supernatural powers and abilities, even though many people are attracted to them.

A man who had returned from a sightseeing trip to Mt. Diamond said to the Founding Master, "While I was traveling around the mountain, I saw a man who was able to call or send away crows or snakes at will. It seemed to me that he was

---

22. *The Scriptures of Won-Buddhism*, 344-345.

a man truly enlightened to the Way." The Founding Master said, "A crow must flock together with crows and a snake must join with snakes. Why should a man enlightened to the Way be among crows or snakes?" The man asked again, "Then what kind of person is truly enlightened to the Way?" The Founding Master said, "A real person of the Way simply follows the Way of a human being amid other humans." The man asked, "If that's the case, then aren't there any distinguishing traits of a person of the Way?" The Founding Master said, "No, there aren't." The man asked, "Then, how do we recognize a person of the Way?" The Founding Master said, "If you are not a person of the Way yourself, it will be hard to recognize one even if you see them. Only if you speak a foreign language well, can you tell whether or not another person speaks that language well. Only if you know music well, can you tell whether another person's music is well played or not. Therefore, it is said that it takes one to know one."[23]

As one progresses on the journey of mind practice, obstacles like biased practice, hasty mind, or the danger of getting caught in the intermediate level may arise for any practitioner.

It is important to understand that if one falls into any of these pitfalls, one cannot become a great dharma vessel and therefore can neither attain great enlightenment, nor truly help this

---

23. Ibid, 232-233.

world. Such a person tends to remain stuck inside these obstacles and continue to commit transgressions. This not only leads to ruining one's own practice, but also to ruining that of others. All practitioners must pay more attention to and be wary of these hindrances.

The Ultimate Key to Success in Practice

Even when we do decide to sincerely follow a spiritual path, we should not forget that the path will not be quick or easy. A few years ago, my niece who lived in Seoul, Korea lost her dog. She used to keep the dog inside her apartment, but one day it went missing. She thought the dog may have escaped the apartment building through an elevator. My brother, sister-in-law, nephew, and niece all looked for the dog. They asked the janitors in the apartment building, people in other apartment complexes, and veterinarians that were nearby. They also posted pictures of the dog with their contact information at shopping centers in case someone saw him. However, they did not hear from anyone for many days.

My niece walked around the neighborhood day and night with the dog's picture, asking whomever she met if they had seen him. For a whole week she walked through the neighborhood in her free time, from early morning till dark. After two weeks, someone told her they had seen a picture of the dog posted by a janitor in one of the nearby apartment compounds. My niece was then finally able to be reunited with her dear pet.

We try to accomplish our goals in many different ways, such as looking to the wisdom and knowledge of others, or praying for help. However, the most fundamental ingredients for success in accomplishing our goals are dedication and commitment.

Just like my niece's sincere dedication to get her dog back motivated her to do many things, great dedication and commitment enabled all enlightened teachers and masters to persevere through many hardships in their quest for the truth.

In the early 1980's, when I was a high school student, not many books were available to study English. For the university entrance exams, most students studied the same book: Sungmoon Comprehensive English.

One day my cousin asked me how many times he should read and study Sungmoon Comprehensive English. I told him that he should read and study the book as many times as it takes for him to understand the contents. If he could understand the book in three readings, three times was enough. If necessary, he should read it as many as thirty times in case there was anything still left that he did not understand.

There is a universal truth that blindly striving for a goal does not guarantee success. We need to reflect on whether the goal we would like to accomplish is truthful and virtuous or not. If the goal is not virtuous or truthful, it is undesirable to make any effort in achieving it. The reason being, if the goal is attained, it still would not guarantee happiness or spiritual progress.

Therefore, we should first set a sincere, righteous goal in our life.

After setting the virtuous goal, we need to keep on diligently working until we achieve it. Depending on the dedication and degree of our effort, it can take a few years, or even decades to finally achieve our goal. But as long as we do not give up hope, and continue to practice with great dedication and focus, we will eventually be successful.

Can you imagine the world without light bulbs? Edison conducted more than 6,000 experiments with various kinds of filaments until he eventually invented the light bulb that we currently use today. He viewed his 5,999 unsuccessful experiments not as failures, but as a process to go through in order to achieve success.

Goethe, who is considered as one of the greatest minds in history, finished writing Faust in his sixties, although he started working on it when he was just in his twenties. Just like many masterpieces in the world, Faust was completed after numerous revisions over his lifetime.

Many people seem reluctant to persevere through hard times when they walk on the dharma path. In a society where efficiency is emphasized and instant foods are popular, we have become impatient; we expect everything quicker than people ever did in the past. A hasty and impatient mind is one of the biggest obstacles for practitioners. Beautiful roses and their fragrance cannot be reconstituted from a package like instant food. It is a universal law of nature that everything takes time and effort, especially something that is important and meaningful. Flowers take time to bloom. Much like blossoming, every goal takes time to be achieved. If something seems to take too much time to be accomplished, it would be helpful to first reflect on whether or not it is in accordance with the law of the universe. Then see if we have the same degree of patience and endurance Edison had when he invented the electric light bulb.

There is a saying "Man proposes, God disposes." All we can do is to keep on working, with great sincerity, dedication, and commitment until we harvest the fruits of our practice.

Il-Won-Sang and
The Goal of Our Life

Socrates said, "Know thyself." Trying to change our environment to create happiness without knowing the reality of our mind is like building a house on quicksand, and expecting to live in it forever. Happiness, suffering, freedom, dissatisfaction, depression, and joy are all words that describe our state of mind. When we clearly see into the reality of our minds, the roots of our suffering are severed, and as a result, suffering ends. The happiness or freedom that comes from the realization of our true self is perpetual and indestructible. In contrast, the happiness that comes from our changing environment is conditional and fragile, and therefore, cannot be everlasting.

If what we want most is not momentary happiness but eternal happiness, then what could be more urgent and important than carrying out spiritual practice in order to realize our true nature? That is why we need to give rise to a great vow to attain great enlightenment and continue to practice.

The Founding Master addressed Yi Tongjinhwa, "Among the many things that a person born into this world should do, there are two that are most essential. The first is to find a teacher of the right-dharma in order to attain Buddhahood. The other is to deliver all sentient beings after being enlightened to the way. These two are the greatest and most essential tasks one can undertake."[24]

There once was a college student who was self-conscious and vulnerable to other people's opinions. Whenever he took an exam, he was extremely worried that he would not do his best. Then, in his sophomore year, he became involved in a student movement whose ideology was based upon socialism. He finally felt that he had found his life goal. Then suddenly, he became focused and tranquil, ceasing to be nervous or worry about the opinions of others. He did not practice meditation—his tranquility and calm state of mind came from his clear life goal.

In the Diamond Sutra, the Buddha first asks all practitioners to make a vow before practice. This vow, or the articulation of life goal, centers and focuses the practitioners' minds:

> One of the disciples asked, "By what method should I cultivate so that I may eliminate all of the five desires, focus single-mindedly on cultivating the Way, and lead a life of tranquility and comfort like the Buddha?" The Founding Master replied, "Rather than eliminating desires, you should expand

[24]. Ibid, 236-237.

them. Once your petty desires are transformed into a great vow, they will naturally subside as you focus single-mindedly on your vow. Then, you will inevitably lead a life of tranquility and comfort."[25]

Saint Paul made tents for a living. The philosopher Spinoza polished eyeglasses to make ends meet. However, no one identifies Saint Paul or Spinoza as a tentmaker or an eyeglass polisher. Likewise, our authentic occupation is to discover our true self and attain Buddhahood. People are engaged in various professions and activities, but our authentic occupation is always the same: attaining supreme enlightenment. Our secular job in the mundane world is simply to make ends meet. We need to clearly understand what is primary and what is secondary in our lives. Our life goal should not be directed toward making more money, possessing more things, or gaining more recognition or fame. Our goal or final destination is reaching nirvana. Therefore, we need to establish and articulate a new life goal and must live with a new value system.

Jesus said, "What good is it to gain the whole world if you lose your soul?" (Matthew 16:26; Mark 8:36). It is time that we embark on the pathless path back to our original mind.

Establishing and articulating a new life goal does not

---

[25]. Ibid, 169.

necessarily mean that people must become monks or nuns in order to seriously practice; as the Buddha did when he left the palace, leaving behind his wife and son. Having a new life goal means having a new value system and living our daily lives with mindfulness.

True practitioners live mindfully. When you have available time, what do you do? Do you watch TV or read magazines, or do you read scripture or practice meditation? How do you spend your time on weekends? Do you go to the movies, or meet friends, or do you meditate or go to dharma service? When you have money and can afford a vacation, what do you do? Do you go to a meditation retreat, or do you go skiing or relax on a beach?

For true practitioners, the criteria used to choose an occupation is also different. They do not choose occupations based on how much money they will make. Rather, they consider whether the occupation in question is a "right livelihood" and whether the work atmosphere is supportive to encouraging spiritual progress.

Saint Francis said, "You are what you seek." Our life goal or our vow for eternal life is like roots. It is the foundation of our practice. Like roots, our vow grows and strengthens. Just as we plant, water, and nurture a seed, our vow is something that we must take care of in order for it to grow. That is why in Mahayana temples, people chant the Four Great Vows at every service.

The Four Great Vows are:

1. Sentient beings are numberless. We vow to save them all.
2. Delusions are endless. We vow to extinguish them all.
3. The teachings are infinite. We vow to learn them all.
4. The Buddha Way is supreme. We vow to attain it.

When the Buddha left his palace, he made two vows: he would attain supreme enlightenment and he would then deliver all sentient beings from suffering. Because of these vows, any time the Buddha sat, he sat with all sentient beings. When he ate, he ate with all sentient beings.

Just like the Buddha, if we practice with such a great vow, then when we sit, we sit with all sentient beings; when we eat, we nourish all sentient beings. Practicing with such a great vow is as powerful as any politician's actions to disarm the military or help hungry children. Bodhisattvas are sometimes called *mahasattvas*, or "great beings," not only because their enlightenment is deep, but also because their vow is great and boundless.

It is not only Nelson Mandela or Martin Luther King, Jr., who are bodhisattvas. If we make this great vow, we all become bodhisattvas, mahasattvas. It is not just Gandhi or Mother Teresa who are holy. As long as we have the great vow, we too are holy. A holy person is not necessarily one who meditates for ten or twelve hours each day. A holy person is not one who practices in the Himalayas. A holy person is one who has made a holy vow and lives according to that vow, always practicing to fulfill it.

Living a holy life in a secular world is far more difficult and far more holy.[26]

Several years ago, a bridge collapsed during rush hour because it could not bear the weight of so much traffic. The investigation revealed that it happened because an engineer had miscalculated the weight of the traffic. One person's carelessness led to a great tragedy, and many lives were lost.

These days, everyone is very closely linked. One person's problem can become a problem for someone else, and one nation's problem can become a global problem. We cannot live or prosper by ourselves. Without the help of others, we cannot survive. Whether we like it or not, we are deeply indebted and connected to others, and we have to live and work together.

Let us all plant the seed of a great vow to be enlightened to ultimate reality—the truth of Il-Won—and to deliver all sentient beings. This is why Sotaesan asked his students to chant the Il-Won-Sang Vow every day. This is why, in every Won Buddhist service, we still chant the Il-Won-Sang Vow.

---

26. Dosung Yoo, *Thunderous Silence*, 34.

CHAPTER 4

THE VIEW OF BIRTH AND DEATH IN WON BUDDHISM

What is Birth and Death?

When people are asked what happens after they die, their answers can be very diverse. Some may say that they are not sure. Others may say that it is the beginning of a new life, or they are going to heaven, or that everything ends after death.

While there are some who possess the extraordinary ability to read their past lives as well as their future lives, most of us don't know for certain what happens after death, or what will happen in our next life.

Whether we are interested in this or not, or have a certain belief or not, the universal fundamental question remains: what if our death is not the end, and how we live our life now greatly influences our future life?

In Korea, during the Chosun Dynasty, there was a good-natured servant named Mungbawoo. One morning, as he was sweeping the court, Mungbawoo saw his friend passing by. "Where are you going?" Mungbawoo asked. "To the market," his friend replied. Mungbawoo then mindlessly followed his friend to the market. As time passed, Mungbawoo's master was annoyed at being unable to find his servant for the entire day. When

Mungbawoo came back near sunset, the master asked him, "Where have you been?" "At the market," Mungbawoo replied. "Why did you go there?" the master asked. "I just followed my friend," Mungbawoo answered. The master said, "You are such an idiot. Didn't it occur to you to let me know where you were going and when you were coming back?" After scolding Mungbawoo, the master gave him a wooden club and said, "From now on, you need to wear this club around your waist. Only when you find someone who is more stupid than you are, can you pass this club on to them." After that, the good-natured Mungbawoo always wore the club around his waist. It was very cumbersome and the club always got in his way as he moved. He couldn't wait to find someone who was stupider than he was so that he could hand it over.

Several years later, the aged master became very ill and was lying on his deathbed. The whole family gathered around him, and believed that he might die at any moment. Tears fell from Mungbawoo's eyes at the thought of losing his master, whom he had served his entire life. Mungbawoo asked, "Master, where will you be going now?" "I don't know," the master replied. "When are you coming back?" Mungbawoo asked. "I don't know," the master replied. At that moment, Mungbawoo wiped his tears and said, "Master, I finally found someone who is stupider than I am. You!" he said, and he handed the wooden club back to his master.

This parable highlights the tendency of people to go about

their busy lives without ever knowing who they are, where they came from, or where they are headed. You may be the world's best driver, but if you do not know your destination, then driving is meaningless. This situation is similar to drifting in a vast ocean, unaware of your direction, even while rowing yourself to exhaustion. This strenuous effort will not get you anywhere. If we do not know our true self, where we have come from, or where we are going, we will fare no better than Mungbawoo.

The Founding Master said, "Ordinary people think that only the present life is important. However, enlightened people regard death to be just as important as their present life. This is because they understand the principle that those who die well will have a good rebirth, and those who live well are better prepared to die well. Birth is the origin of death, and death is the origin of birth. Thus, it is wise to prepare for death during one's whole life. However, after forty, it becomes especially important to begin preparing for death's approach so one does not need to rush at the last moments."

"The birth and death of human beings can be likened to blinks of the eye, to inhalation and exhalation of breath, and to falling into sleep and awakening. Except for the difference in length of time, the principle is the same: birth and death are not two. Originally, nothing is born or perishes. Therefore, the enlightened person regards it as change, but the unenlightened person regards it as birth and death."

"People generally call the world we live in 'this world' and the world where the dead go the 'other world.' They presume that 'this world' and the 'other world' are separate realms. However, it is only the body and its location that change; these are not separate worlds."[1]

"Both sentient and insentient beings in this world all possess the element of life. Nothing is completely annihilated but merely goes through a change of form. For example, a decomposing human corpse makes the soil rich and as a result the spot will be thick with grass. The grass can be made into compost when mowed. This, in turn, is used as fertilizer that the crop will absorb and yield grains. The grains then become the blood and flesh of human beings, helping maintain human life and actions. If one looks at it from such a perspective, then nothing in the universe perishes forever. Even a single straw will manifest itself into a hundred million transformations and will itself create and exhibit various manifestations. Therefore, you must inquire deeply into this principle and awaken to the truth that all things in the universe sustain endless lives through the principle of 'neither arising nor ceasing.'"[2]

A traveler was walking in a field when, suddenly, the field caught fire and a wild elephant began to chase him. He ran for his life and finally escaped to a tall tree at the edge of a cliff. He hung tightly to a vine because at the base of the tree the elephant

---

1. *The Scriptures of Won-Buddhism*, 316-325.
2. *The Scripture of Wonbulkyo*, 292-293.

waited for him. Then, looking over the edge of the cliff, he saw a deep abandoned well with five slithering snakes below. He could neither jump down, nor climb back up. As time passed, he became exhausted, clinging to the vine. To make things worse, as evening approached and darkness set in, two rats, one white and one black, appeared on the tree and began to gnaw at the vine. The traveler knew that if he jumped down into the well, he would be bitten by the snakes. At the same time, if he climbed down the tree to the field, he would be killed by the elephant. He did not know what to do and desperately contemplated his situation. Then, he saw honey dripping from an empty beehive on the tree. Forgetting his situation entirely, he started to lick and enjoy the honey.

Here, the traveler represents a person who is born into this world. The field represents life, and the elephant symbolizes death or impermanence. The five snakes represent the five aggregates that comprise a human: our physical body, sensations, perceptions, impulses and consciousness. The white and black rats symbolize both day and night, and the change of time. Honey symbolizes worldly pleasures.

If you are a soccer player and want your team to win the game, you need to practice diligently beforehand. Similarly, without practice or preparation, we cannot expect to perform well. The birth and death of humans is like the arising and ceasing of our thoughts and emotions. When we study the Buddhadharma and train ourselves to attain freedom of mind, we then can ultimately attain great enlightenment and liberation from the cycle of birth and death.

In order to attain freedom of mind and eternal life, the practitioner needs to prepare the following.

Preparation for One's Future Life

The Vow

To make a vow is to make a commitment. A vow in Buddhism is an unwavering oath, a sacred aspiration or a strong determination to attain great enlightenment for the benefit of all sentient beings.

A vow is offered to the realm of Truth as well as to the Buddhas and sages across time. A vow is the path to a pure, altruistic way of life beyond one's selfish desires and attachments.

Nobody has ever attained Buddhahood without first making a great vow.

Making a vow is akin to planting the seed of Buddhahood. This seed, under the right conditions, will eventually transform into a huge tree in whose shade all sentient beings can rest. By giving rise to a great vow, one's mind becomes consolidated and empowered. The practitioner gains the strength to overcome all kinds of obstacles. Great faith and dedication arises from an unshakable vow.

"Occasionally, a person will experience their first glimpse of awakening without fully understanding their own spiritual capacity. This drives them to intensify their methods of practice in order to reach enlightenment. However, if one practices with that state of mind, one becomes susceptible to physical ailments, or will lose interest when awakening is not achieved quickly. This causes a change in their mind and they may turn away from a life of cultivating the Way. This is something to be wary of. There are also those who reach the ground of Buddhahood in a single leap. These are people of superior capacity who have practiced over many lifetimes. Those of middle and lesser capacity must work hard to accumulate the merits of practice for a long period of time. The proper sequence of practice necessary to attain enlightenment begins with establishing a great vow. After establishing a great vow, a great belief arises, followed by great courage, then great questioning and great dedication. Only after great dedication will a great awakening occur. Keep in mind that awakening and awareness will not happen all at once, but that the process involves thousands upon thousands of insights before attaining great enlightenment."[3]

A vow is the motivating force that enables all practitioners to attain Buddhahood. It works like an accelerator pedal, increasing our speed as we travel on the steep and challenging path towards Buddhahood. This vow is like a shield which can cast off temptations and obstacles and acts as a drill that can penetrate through

3. Ibid, 168.

all barriers.

With a great vow, the practitioner's life goal becomes clear. Possessing a vow or not is what differentiates the average person from a great practitioner or saint.

Jesus said, "You are in this world, but you are not of this world."

It is not easy to live apart from others, nor to live with a different mindset from those who are not seekers of the way. However, if we live mindlessly and follow the majority's value system, our final destination will be far from attaining freedom of mind. All practitioners should have a clear understanding that with the support of dharma friends and teachers, the path to nirvana becomes far easier. With their help, we can easily overcome a multitude of temptations and hindrances.

Physical closeness does not make people true companions. It is by making the same vows to attain great enlightenment for the benefit of all sentient beings that they can become true dharma friends. These are dharma friends who walk together along the same path to Buddhahood. At times, practitioners may enter a state of confusion and become lost on their path to Buddhahood. However, by recalling and reestablishing their vow, they can quickly return to their dharma path, especially during times of difficulty.

When practicing with an unshakable vow, we become like a boat receiving light from a lighthouse when lost in the vast ocean. It is like a torch which leads the wandering soul out of the labyrinth. Thus, by making a great vow, one can eventually become free from the burden of ignorance and can dissolve the barriers of one's karma. Without a strong vow, great courage, passion, and zeal will not arise. When one's vow and actions are aligned, they act as fertile soil where the seeds of Buddhahood can be planted, and obstacles on one's path can be removed.

The Master Chongsan, the Second Head Dharma Master of Won Buddhism, continued expounding on external concentration-calmness and internal concentration-calmness. "External concentration-calmness is the practice of keeping one's resolution externally immovable as follows. First, one develops a great aspiration. This unwavering aspiration allows one to see without hindrance amidst the multitude of worldly experience that one encounters. Just as the pleasure of the royal palace or the suffering of the Himalayas did not stay in the mind of Śākyamuni once he resolved to attain the great Way."[4]
"It is not my instruction to have you eliminate by force your feelings of joy or anger, sorrow or happiness. Rather, I urge you to exercise your free frame of mind without constraint by applying joy, anger, sorrow, and happiness properly, according to time and place, only making sure that you do not diverge from the Middle Way. Instead of resenting mediocre talent and petty desires, worry instead that your own talent and aspiration are not great. Therefore, the dharma I teach is meant only

4. Ibid, 865.

to enlarge what is small and to redirect practitioners' efforts away from things that are petty and guide each toward things that are great. This is in fact the great dharma that achieves great things."[5]

Master Chongsan said:

"The greatest of all aspirations in the world is the four great vows. You take the vow to save innumerable sentient beings. In order to realize this vow, you eradicate all defilement from your mind without ceasing, learn the Dharma teaching with utmost sincerity, and continue to cultivate the Way of the Buddha throughout your eternal life. Then you will accomplish the great vow to realize Buddhahood and save sentient beings. The difference between buddha-bodhisattvas and ordinary sentient beings is like that between a huge tree and a seedling. The little seedling will be a huge tree when it has grown; a sentient being becomes a buddha-bodhisattva with continuous practice. Therefore, if you have an unwavering will to do something, then you can do it, no matter how difficult it is. However, if you are unwilling to do anything, nothing will be accomplished. If, understanding that the Buddha and you are not two, you steadily cultivate the Way with the four great vows, there will be nothing that cannot be accomplished."[6]

5. Ibid, 164.
6. Ibid, 907.

In *The Sutra of Forty-Two*, Section 42, the Buddha said, "I look upon royalty and their highest ranking dignitaries as I would upon the dust that floats in a sunbeam through a crack. I consider treasures of gold and jade equal to brick and broken tiles. I look upon clothing of fine silk as I would upon old worn cotton."

Unwavering Faith

Strong, unwavering faith is essential for our practice. The Buddha said, "One can enter the ocean of dharma only through faith."

When carrying out spiritual mind practice, faith plays a crucial role in freeing us from perpetual suffering and liberation from the endless cycle of birth and death.

Sotaesan said faith is the "motivating force that settles the mind when one tries to accomplish anything."

The Founding Master said, "The reason faith is considered the most important of all assets in the Order of Moral Training is that faith is the vessel that contains the dharma, the basic power by which koans are solved and the basis for keeping the Precepts. Studying and practicing without faith is equivalent to watering dead plants: there are no results. Therefore, first establish a stable faith and then you can save yourself. The important thing in teaching others is to evoke faith from people with no faith."[7]

Hearing that Song Hyon-pung was studying the prospect of an unlimited power source, Master Chongsan said, "Machines may need unlimited power, but our cultivation of the Way also needs unlimited power. The unlimited power of cultivating the Way is belief and dedication. Those are the power sources that turn ordinary people into sages."[8]

Only those who have strong faith can reap the harvest of spiritual mind practice and be guided after their death.

Sotaesan said, "The most urgent matter is not to teach everyone numerous scriptures or to encourage them to perform thousands of good deeds. The most urgent matter is to help people believe in and awaken to the truth of neither arising nor ceasing and the karmic principle of cause and effect."[9]

"The truth of neither arising nor ceasing" refers to eternal life. How do so many people sincerely trust the karmic principle of cause and effect, or in the belief that we reap exactly what we sow?

Without having or trusting a map, one cannot embark on the journey to nirvana. The words of the Buddha compose the map needed for our journey. Without faith to walk the dharma path to attaining eternal life, we will not be amply motivated.

---

7. *The Scriptures of Won-Buddhism*, 347.
8. *The Scripture of Wonbulkyo*, 875.
9. Ibid, 225-226.

Sotaesan said:

"Though the spring breeze blows impartially without any thought of self, only living trees can receive its energy and grow; though sages give dharma impartially without any thought of self, only people with belief can receive that dharma completely."[10]

Without faith in universal truth and the teachings of the buddhas, one lacks firm determination to practice, and encounters many internal and external obstacles.

A mature practitioner's mind is like a tree whose roots have grown deeply into the Earth. Their mind will not waver despite strong winds or difficult situations. The practitioner's mind must root itself deeply into the teachings of the buddhas who have attained great enlightenment and thus clearly know the path to liberation. Among practitioners there are many levels of faith.

Master Chongsan said:

"The roots of faith vary in depth. If you are drawn to various theories and assertions without a fixed view of your own, and are shaken hither and thither, ruining your life by acting as you please, the root of your faith is as unstable as falling leaves. If you have firm faith in the true dharma, such that your faith is not shaken by minor adverse conditions but is shaken by

---

10. *The Scriptures of Won-Buddhism*, 349.

major ones, though you do not become depraved, the root of your faith is like that of a tree. If your faith is deep such that you are never shaken by any adverse circumstances or difficult situation, such that you do not fall into the suffering of transgression because your conscience leads you, the root of your faith is like that of a huge mountain."[11]

Just as a baby completely trusts their mother when resting at her bosom, when practitioners completely trust the words of the buddha, their minds and hearts unite with their teachers. In Won Buddhism, this level of faith is called *tuck-shin*, which means "special faith."

Daesan, the Third Head Dharma Master of Won Buddhism, said that with "special faith" the tree of supreme enlightenment takes root. Thus, one's progress toward attaining great enlightenment becomes accelerated.

Shin, or faith, is sometimes called *shin-kun*, which translates into "the root of faith." These terms are used interchangeably because faith is the foundation of the practice of all practitioners, just as the root is the foundation of a tree.

Just as a root continuously grows, our faith or belief also grows and strengthens. The more we understand the dharma, the more we practice. The more we associate with our teachers and dharma friends, the deeper and firmer our faith becomes.

---

11. Ibid, 870-871.

With this kind of deep faith, we can overcome various obstacles and quickly move toward our destination to nirvana or liberation from the cycle of life and death.

Power of the Mind

There is a saying, "Cultivation of the mind for three days will last for a thousand years, but material things amassed for a hundred years will crumble into dust in one morning."

This means that the value of cultivating one's mind is not short-lived, but rather, has a truly lasting impact and benefit for all of one's life. In contrast, material gains may be easily lost and can become meaningless over a short period of time. It is unfortunate that despite these truths, many people work their entire lives to attain things without lasting value.

In *The Sutra of Forty-Two Sections*, Section 11, the Buddha said:

"To feed one hundred bad men is not equal to feeding one good one. To feed one thousand good men is not equal to feeding one who observes the five precepts. Feeding ten thousand who observe the five precepts is not equal to feeding one Srotaapana. Feeding one million Srotaapanas is not equal to feeding one Sakrdagamin. Feeding ten million Sakrdagamins is not equal to feeding one Anagamin. Feeding one hundred million Anagamins is not equal to feeding one Arhat. Feeding one thousand million Arhats is not equal to feeding one

Pratyeka Buddha. Feeding ten thousand million Pratyeka Buddhas is not equal to feeding one of the buddhas of the Triple World. Feeding one hundred million buddhas of the triple worlds is not equal to realizing one's true nature where there is nothing to cultivate, nothing to attain."

When we contemplate the reality of the endless cycle of birth and death for all human beings, spiritual practice becomes critically important.

Master Daesan said, "Well-ripened persimmons fall, but unripened ones fall as well. Everyone dies eventually; therefore, everyone should practice and prepare for their death and for their next life."

The first emperor in China, Qin (259-210 BC), possessed great power. It is said that his power was even strong enough to stop the sun from setting. In order to preserve his life, he sent five hundred young men and women to a faraway land in search of the 'Elixir of Immortality.' Yet, despite his power and wealth, he still could not avoid death. At the time of his death, the superior power with which he had ruled his empire was just as ineffective as a piece of discarded straw. Even heroes and celebrities will eventually turn into ashes.

One young Won Buddhist minister, while studying for his doctoral degree, found that he had cancer. Facing this unexpected disastrous situation, he said to his dharma friends, "I should have known how crucial and imminent the matter of life and death is. If I knew, I would not have wasted so much time studying for my academic degree. As a result, I am not well prepared for my next life."

People try hard in their life to attain fame or wealth. Yet, this will be all in vain if they have not carried out spiritual practice based on a great vow to prepare for eternal life.

Sotaesan said:

"No matter how much a person might have accumulated grains and money throughout his life, he cannot take anything with him when he dies. How can we call that which we cannot take along with us our eternal possessions? If we want to create eternal possessions, then while we are alive we must work hard for others' benefit in every possible way, but must do so without dwelling on any sign that benefit is conferred so that we may accumulate merit that is free from the outflows. Our true, eternal possession is the vow regarding the right dharma and the power of the mind that has cultivated it. By devoting ceaseless efforts to this vow and to mind practice, we will become a master of wisdom and merit in the infinite world."[12]

People may love their family members dearly and be willing to do anything for them, but still, they cannot die in their place. Death is an exclusively personal matter. It cannot be shared with anyone.

12. Ibid, 328.

One enlightened master said, "No matter how many loved ones you have around you, or how many valuables you possess, you cannot take them with you to your next life. The journey to death is a solitary road that must be taken all by oneself."

While in exile for three years in Kueichow, Wang Yang-ming (1472-1529), a prominent Confucian scholar, built a stone gazebo and devoted himself to spiritual practice. He eventually reached the state of freedom from the desire for worldly fame and wealth. However, he was not able to liberate himself from the matter of life and death.

One day, he visited a nearby Buddhist monastery and asked whether there was anything extraordinary about the monastery. One monk replied, "There is a cabin behind this monastery and about forty years ago, a monk entered it. Since he entered the cabin, no one has been able to open the door, though many have tried."

Wang thought that was very odd, so he went to the cabin and tried to open the door. Strangely enough, the door opened very easily. Inside the cabin, he saw a dead monk in a seated meditation posture. The dead body was completely dry and mummified. On the wall was written, "This is Wang Shou-jen. The person who closed the door will be the one who opens it. One's spirit does not die, but comes back again. This is the everlasting dharma body."

Having read these lines, Wang realized that he was the monk who had entered the hermitage in his previous life and had written the poem. It is said that when Wang read that poem, he attained enlightenment and was finally able to liberate himself from life and death.

The Founding Master addressed the congregation at a New Year's Day ceremony saying, "There is nothing special about either yesterday or today, but everything through yesterday we call 'last year' and from today forward we call it 'this year'. Similarly, it is the same spirit when we die as it is when we are alive, but we call where one goes after death the 'other world,' and when one is alive, we call it 'this world.' The physical body, composed of the four great elements of earth, water, fire, and wind, has a 'this world' and an 'other world' because it dissipates and is reborn. However, the spirit is eternally inextinguishable and thus never subject to birth or death. Therefore, for the enlightened, birth, old age, sickness, and death are like the changing of the four seasons, and the difference between what we call 'this world' and the 'other world' is like that of last year and this year."
Chŏng Ilsŏng asked the Founding Master, "When my life is coming to an end, what final thought should I maintain?" The Founding Master responded, "Rest in clear awareness." Chŏng asked again, "What is the road of death and rebirth like?" The Founding Master replied, "It is like falling asleep and then waking up. Falling asleep you are unconscious of yourself, but when you wake up, you find you are that same Ilsŏng again. This existence called Ilsŏng is endlessly reborn and dies again

according to his karma."[13]

The power cultivated through one's mind practice is the only means of solving the crucial matter of life and death. No one can create this state for another. It may be nice to have many mourners at one's funeral service, but one cannot bring anything or anyone into their next life.

There was a well-known Korean millionaire in his late sixties, who had surgery to remove a cancerous tumor. It was his third operation since developing cancer some years earlier. After the surgery, he asked the surgeon in charge how it went and what the prospects were for his recovery. The doctor candidly told him that since the cancer was so widespread, it would be hard for him to recover completely. Although this news had been expected, the millionaire was still very upset. To regain composure, he went to the bathroom to brush his teeth and wash his face. As he raised his toothbrush, he had the profound realization that he could not even take the simple toothbrush with him when he left this world.[14]

The bible says, "Vanity of vanities, says the Preacher; Vanity of vanities, all is vanity." (Ecclesiastes 1:1-2).

Many people make plans as if they will live for thousands of

---

13. Ibid, 325-328.
14. Dosung Yoo, *Thunderous Silence*, 234.

years. Material things are amassed in vain. They are like the dew on grass, like a candle in the wind, a shadow or a bubble.

Master Chongsan said:

"A deer loved her magnificent antlers, but was ashamed of her ugly-looking legs. One day, being chased by a hunter as she was escaping danger through the bush, her magnificent horns impeded her escape but her unsightly legs ran well and saved her life. Although this is only a fable, if we reflect on our own circumstances, we can say that this is a cautionary tale that clearly depicts the state of our world."[15]

We should not waste our time in search of worldly things. Nor should we postpone making preparations for our death. Instead, we should diligently practice to attain eternal life.

One should prepare to undertake this critical journey courageously in daily life by practicing diligently to attain the Three Great Powers of the mind: the Power of Spiritual Cultivation, the Power of Wisdom and Inquiry, and the Power of Choice in Action.

Once we have developed these three great powers sufficiently, there will be nothing in this world that we cannot handle. Eventually, freedom from birth and death and liberation from the cycle of rebirth will become possible for us.

The Threefold Practice represents the fundamentals of our

---

15. *The Scripture of Wonbulkyo*, 930.

spiritual life as we carry out mind practice.

Master Chwasan, the Fourth Head Dharma Master of Won Buddhism, said that the Threefold Practice represents "three great veins of ore" wherein we can locate our spiritual treasures. As we dig deeper, we find countless precious jewels. The three veins of Spiritual Cultivation, Cultivation of Wisdom and Inquiry, and Choice in Action represent a place where a limitless bounty of treasure awaits.

If we practice intently and consistently according to the Threefold Practice, we will eventually attain freedom of mind and be able to liberate ourselves from the cycle of life and death.

Sotaesan said:

"If one always exerts oneself with utmost sincerity to keeping one's mind free from being disturbed, to keep one's mind free from being deluded, and to keep one's mind-ground free from being defiled, then, with that power, one will acquire the ability to deliver even the sentient beings in hell. By creating even just once an affinity with the right dharma of the buddhas, a wholesome seed will be planted for attaining Buddhahood during or after this lifetime."[16]

Tae-Go asked, "Can people's spirits be sent on only after death?" Sotaesan responded, "As far as sending on the spirit is concerned, there is no difference between birth and death.

---

16. Ibid, 298.

Thus, rather than someone else sending on your spirit after your death, it is more effective if you send on your own spirit while you are alive. Discipline your mind every day to be bright, well-kept, and upright, so when the six consciousnesses are in contact with the six sense objects, they do not become either disturbed or polluted. Then, you will not only attain the great ability to deliver others, but may also complete your own deliverance while you are alive. Unfortunately, there are few people who possess this ability. That is why practitioners throughout the three time-periods have assiduously strived to cultivate the Way."[17]

Carrying out the Threefold Practice to prepare for eternal life by freeing ourselves from the cycle of birth and death is not easy. Such practice requires patience and perseverance.

Zhang Liang was a military officer who descended from an aristocratic family of a country destroyed by the Emperor Qin Shi Huang in 221 BC. Thereafter, Zhang Liang made plans to assassinate Qin Shi Hung and reestablish his home state. However, he failed in a poorly planned attack upon the carriage of Qin Shi Huang and became a fugitive, wandering around with a fake identity.

One day, he saw an old man sitting on a bridge in a small village near the countryside. The old man asked Zhang Liang

[17]. Ibid, 304.

to fetch his shoes that had fallen under the bridge. Zhang Liang went under the bridge and picked up the shoes for the old man as requested. Then the old man asked Zhang Liang to put the shoes on him. Zhang Liang politely put the shoes on, but the old man shook his feet so one shoe would fall back under the bridge. Once again, the old man told Zhang Liang to retrieve the shoe for him. Though Zhang Liang got upset with the old man, he obeyed him with great endurance and perseverance.

Next, the old man praised him and said he wanted to see him the next day so he could give him a present.

When Zhang Liang came back to the bridge the next day, the old man was already waiting for him and scolded him, "A young man should come before an old man." He then told Zhang Liang to come back the next day.

When Zhang Liang came to the bridge early the next morning, the old man was already there and said the same thing.

Frustrated, Zhang Liang decided not to leave the bridge and waited till sunset for the old man to return. It was just when Zhang Liang was about to give up waiting and leave that the old man arrived and gave him a book. He said, "You'd better read this book if you want to unify the world." Then the old man disappeared.

Surprised that the old man knew his ambition, Zhang Liang read and studied the book countless times.

Years later, Zhang Laing went back to find the old man, but instead found a large yellow rock where he had sat. As a result, the old man became known as Huang Shigong (黃石公; lit. "Yellow

Rock Old Man"). The book that many believe the old man gave Zhang Laing is called *Soshu* (素書), which is known as "The Book of Secret Teachings." This book is one of the great ancient Chinese books about mind training and wisdom taught from the perspective of a military strategy.

Zhang Liang dedicated himself to studying the book, training, and cultivating his mind. Among many lessons he learned, he regarded the importance of patience, planning, and preparation to be the most significant.

Eventually, Zhang Liang would greatly contribute to the founding of the Han Dynasty, and become known as one of the greatest heroes in Chinese history.

Eating a spoonful of soup does not make us full. Yet, if we continue to eat spoon by spoon, we will become full. Likewise, when we carry out the Threefold Practice regularly with great patience, we will eventually strengthen our minds and attain liberation from the cycle of birth and death.

The Blessing of Generosity

A meritorious act of generosity is one that is performed without expecting anything in return. Giving without expecting a reward will truly benefit people everywhere.

Generosity begins in the mind of an individual who goes beyond their own material desires. Performing meritorious acts for others is the noblest of all human behaviors. This is why the Buddha places Dana paramita as the first paramita. Dana means "generosity," the practice of giving without an expectation of receiving anything in return. Paramita means "perfection," "crossing over," or "going to the other shore (nirvana)." Paramitas are types of training used to perfect or purify ourselves in order to attain enlightenment.

The Buddha taught six paramitas which are necessary to reach that other shore, and to proceed from the world of suffering to the world of freedom.

The root of our desires and our wandering thoughts is our ego. Generosity, especially giving away those things that we cherish, is one of the best and most powerful ways to dissolve our sense of self. Dana is the manifestation of our true self, or no-self. By practicing Dana paramita, we can cultivate *bodhichitta*, which is the aspiration to attain awakening in order to deliver all beings from suffering.

When we practice Dana paramita, and live our lives compassionately, without ego, the nature of our true self is revealed.

According to the Buddha's own words, helping others is also a powerful way of creating blessings, which are important assets for practitioners. Without many blessings, it is hard for us to find an ideal environment to support our practice. Without many blessings, we cannot meet good teachers or good dharma friends. Letting go of self and helping others is not only a great way to dissolve our sense of self, but it is also a great way to create many blessings.

The merits resulting from acts of generosity fall equally upon the giver and the receiver, radiating outward toward all of humanity.

At deliverance ceremonies for the deceased, Dana is an important factor that affects the deliverance of the deceased to a higher realm of existence. Those who have merits and blessings are able to lead a good life, and those merits and blessings will greatly affect their future lives.

One of the disciples asked, "From ancient times there has been a custom of holding a Buddhist service for the spirit of the deceased. In the service, sons, daughters, relatives, and friends make offerings to the Buddha statue or have dharma teachers of high virtue give sermons and recite Buddhist scriptures for the sake of the spirit. How could this service influence the spirit? What difference would the degree of sincerity and the dharma power of the teacher make on the spirit?" Sotaesan replied, "To show one's sincerity to the spirit of the deceased, one holds prayers and makes offerings to the Buddha statue. An old saying goes, 'Sincerity can move heaven.' Thus, the effect of prayers and making offerings to the Buddha statue will be proportional to the degree of sincerity; and the sermon and recitation of the scriptures will have an effect on the spirit proportional to the dharma power of the dharma teacher. Consequently, certain spirits unknowingly enter the virtuous path after settling their past debt or may instantaneously gain freedom and directly return to the virtuous path. Others can be helped to find the right path for the next life, even though they are lost in the intermediate existence between death and reincarnation. Lastly, there are those who attain freedom from momentary attachment, become free and enjoy blessedness in the human and heavenly realms. If, however, the sincerity of the people offering the service for the deceased is not outstanding or the dharma teacher's spiritual power is deficient, it may not have much effect on the spirit. This is because without utmost sincerity and spiritual power, the true potency will not be manifested, just as in farming there will not be much of a crop to harvest without the farmer's full dedication and ability."[18]

Only a practitioner who has accumulated many blessings can attain Buddhahood. A buddha is not a person who simply attains supreme enlightenment. He or she is also one who has accumulated a great number of blessings. Wisdom and blessings are two assets that are necessary to attain Buddhahood.

A traveler needs money to have a comfortable journey and good accommodations. The same is true for us on our journey to death; people need merits and blessings in order to have a good journey. One needs to plant the seeds of merits and blessings by helping others spiritually, physically, or materially.

18. Ibid, 299-300.

Sotaesan said:

"The Truth of the Universe continually involves repetitive and continuous circulation without arising or ceasing. Thus, whatever goes will return again and what comes will depart again. In this revolving continuum, the giver becomes a receiver and a receiver becomes a giver. This is the constant Way that has never changed throughout eternity."[19]

"Plants live by setting their roots in the earth. Once a seed or root is planted in the soil, a new shoot will often sprout. Given the right cause and condition of the season, the plant will continue to grow. Animals, on the other hand, live by setting their roots in heaven. Thus, by thinking one thought, speaking one word or committing one action, creation of a karmic cause in the Dharma realm occurs. In this void of the universe, the karmic retribution of the animal will be imprinted in the universe and appears proportionally to each and every wholesome or unwholesome condition. With this awareness, how then can anyone possibly deceive other human beings or heaven?"[20]

While Master Sotaesan was dwelling at Pongnae hermitage, the wretched shriek of a wild boar shot by a hunter was so pitiful that it prompted the Master to say, "One's gain is

19. Ibid, 291.
20. Ibid, 219-210.

another's loss." He also said, "Witnessing the death of this wild boar, I can surmise its past deeds; and witnessing this hunter slaughtering the wild boar today, I can also surmise what the hunter will face in the future."[21]

Merits we create are stored in a warehouse in heaven, and we will retrieve them in our next life.

In Korean, insufficient merits are referred to as "Kwanchol's Warehouse." This expression originated from the following story.

Kwanchol, a rich Korean man, worked diligently throughout his life in order to accumulate material wealth. After his death, he was brought to Yama, the Lord of the Underworld. He begged Yama to allow him to go back to the world where he had lived. Yama replied, "Only those who have accumulated great merit and many blessings of generosity are able to go back. Why don't you go to your warehouse to see how much merit and blessings you have earned during your life?"

Kwanchol was then taken to a warehouse with his name on the door. However, when he opened the door, the large storage space was entirely empty aside from a bundle of straw in the corner. This was a sharp contrast to the warehouse in his home, which had many bags of grains and valuables. He suddenly recalled that a long time ago, he had given a bundle of straw to a poor woman in his neighborhood, who had just given birth

---

21. Ibid, 223-224.

to a baby in the middle of winter. He had felt sorry for the poor woman and given her the bundle of straw so that she could burn it and keep her room warm.

Kwanchol deeply understood that without accumulating the merit of giving, one's warehouse in heaven will remain empty. He regretted his past actions and begged Yama, "I lived my life satisfying only my own interests. From now on, I will do good things for others and accumulate merit. Please give me one more chance." As a result, Yama granted him his wish.

Kwanchol then returned to the world as a completely different person, and began performing many good deeds for his neighbors.

When one does good things for others, one accumulates merit for oneself. Many people, not understanding this karmic principle of cause and effect, are reluctant to help or to give things to others. Moreover, even when they do so, they hesitate because they feel as though they are losing something that belongs to them. They are like a farmer who keeps seeds in his storage bin because he does not know that his harvest will increase hundredfold if he plants them in the soil.

If you cannot give because you have no possessions, that is a different story. However, if you store things in your warehouse and still do not practice Dana, or the merit of giving, you are not a wise person. You will neither spiritually progress, nor be born in the higher realms of existence in the next life.

Conversely, one should be aware that what one receives from others in this life incurs a debt in the next life; a debt which one must pay back someday.

People often feel happy when they receive things or are helped by others, but they are actually incurring debts from the perspective of eternal life and the universal principle of cause and effect.

One needs both merit and blessings to be born into a good environment and to have a mutually beneficial relationship with their children. The same holds true for our ability to encounter the teachings of buddhas or sages.

Therefore, the more blessings and merits we create, the more abundant our present life and future lives will become.

According to the Diamond Sutra, a person who has attained the Buddha's teachings, especially one who has heard about the Heart Sutra or Diamond Sutra, is someone who has previously planted many meritorious seeds.

> Subhuti said to Buddha: World-honored One, will there always be men who will truly believe after coming to hear these teachings [of the Perfection of Transcendental Wisdom]? Buddha answered: Subhuti, do not utter such words! At the end of the last five-hundred-year period following the passing of the Tathagata, there will be self-controlled men, rooted in merit, coming to hear these teachings, who will be inspired with belief. But you should realize that such men have not strengthened their root of merit under just one Buddha, or two Buddhas, or three, or four, or five Buddhas, but under

countless Buddhas; and their merit is of every kind. Such men, coming to hear these teachings, will have an immediate uprising of pure faith, Subhuti; and the Tathagata will recognize them. Yes, He will clearly perceive all these of pure heart, and the magnitude of their moral excellences.

Without many blessings, it is also hard for us to find an ideal environment that supports our practice, and we may not meet a good teacher or find a good dharma friend.

All practitioners need to create blessings diligently by unselfishly helping others in various ways. This is one of the essential ways for us to free ourselves from the cycle of birth and death.

Chong Myong-do and Chong Lee-chon were very well-known Chinese scholars during China's Song Dynasty. The mother of the Chong brothers sincerely wished to have good sons who would save the nation. One day, while she was working in the field, she felt something hard in the soil at the edge of her hoe. She dug deeper and found a nugget of gold. Most people would have been overjoyed at such unexpected fortune. However, the mother of the Chong brothers shouted towards the sky, "I don't want this lump of gold. All I want are sons who will grow up to be great men."

With these words, she simply buried the gold nugget back in the soil. It is said that shortly after this incident, she gave birth to the Chong brothers.

If she had taken advantage of the situation and used the gold, she may not have given birth to great sons. Because she refused her apparent good fortune and stayed true to her sincere wish, she became the mother of two of the greatest Confucian scholars in the history of China.

Many people keep things of value in storage. As a result, those things become the very cause of their worries. They worry that the items could become damaged, stolen, or destroyed by unexpected events such as fire or flood.

Imagine if we used those assets for the benefit of people who need them instead of worrying. The more we give, the more merits and blessings we will accumulate. All the accumulated blessings will be a great asset to guide our paths in the future.

Everybody wants a good family, good health, a loving partner, and to ultimately lead a happy life. However, contrary to their desire, people often create unwholesome karma, which leads them in the opposite direction from what they want.

Sotaesan said:

"If a person hasn't created merit, then no matter how well he wishes to do in his next life, it will not turn out that way. This may be compared to a case in the present life where, no matter how much someone wishes to reside in a nice home, one wouldn't be able to live and claim it as his own. Look at Kongch'il! When he gets off at Iri Railway Station, there is a row of fancy Western-style homes. He does not dare even to think of going inside them and goes into his own humble dwelling. This is indeed a living example of how one receives in accordance with what one has created."[22]

Master Haewol, one of the greatest spiritual teachers in Korean history, was well known for cleaning things. When he moved out of a residence, he always left it spotless and freshly painted. He also replaced the wallpaper and planted new trees. One day, someone asked why he spent so much time taking care of a house in which he would no longer live. The Master replied that whenever one left a place, they should always leave behind merit.

Similarly, we should leave merit behind in order to create favorable conditions in our lives and follow the teachings of buddhas or sages.

There is an old Korean saying: A General with great wisdom cannot defeat a General with abundant virtue. A General with great virtue cannot defeat a General with abundant blessings.

One needs blessings in order to carry out spiritual practice without obstacles. Because practitioners with abundant blessings and merits naturally find a supportive sangha, great teachers, and good dharma friends, they can easily devote themselves to spiritual practice.

I still remember what my grandmother told me when I was

---

22. Ibid, 226.

very little. She said, "Even if you have a fancy wedding with a large dowry, you cannot lead a good life if you do not have enough blessings. Even if you have nothing at the beginning of your marriage, but have obtained many blessings, you will lead an abundant life."

We may not be satisfied with our present situation, but if we diligently create blessings and merits by working hard and helping others, then we will eventually encounter favorable situations.

There is another old Korean saying, "Even if you are abandoned on a remote mountain, ravens or magpies will bring you food if you have abundant blessings."

Many people try to save money and deposit it in the bank. As their savings account increases, they feel secure and rewarded for the hard work and difficulties they have endured. However, it is far more important that we save up blessings in our heavenly account for our eternal life.

Jesus said, "Do not store up for yourselves treasures on earth, which moths and vermin destroy, and where thieves break in and steal. Rather, store up for yourselves treasures in heaven, which moths and vermin cannot destroy, and where thieves do not break in and steal. For where your treasure is, there your heart will also be."(Matthew 6:19-21, NIV).

Preparing for a driving test is not the same as preparing for the bar exam. The greater the work, the longer it takes to prepare for it. Whether it involves accumulating blessings or empowering our minds through the Threefold Practice, we need to begin when we are young and healthy; the younger, the better. The best way to achieve success in any area is to prepare in advance.

Deng Xiaoping (1904–1997) was removed from Chinese political circles during the Cultural Revolution. However, he did not lose hope. Instead, he retreated to the countryside, believing in his eventual return. He mapped out his vision and devised plans for a new China in the future. Upon Mao Zedong's death, Deng Xiaoping quickly returned to the political stage and began to implement his plans for China's future.

Everyone aspires to be successful. Moreover, in spiritual practice, we should start preparing for our eternal life as soon as possible.

Letting go of Attachments

When we carry out mind practice, we need to practice letting of go of our attachments. Attachments, wholesome or unwholesome, shackle our mind and deprive us of attaining freedom of mind.

When we consider our eternal life, letting go of our attachments is crucial, especially when facing death.

Sotaesan said:

"When the numinous consciousness departs from the physical body, it first follows that person's attachments, and then acquires a new body in accordance with its karma, thus entering the endless cycle of reincarnation. The only way to become free from this transmigration is to surrender all attachments and thereby transcend karma."[23]

"Everyday people have to practice and train their minds to eliminate attachments. One with strong attachments to property, lovers, fame, profit, family, clothes, food and shelter will suffer from worries and anxieties far more strongly than other people when losing even one of these things. This is hell in real life, and when one is about to die, one will never be free from these attachments, and will fall into the abyss of transgression. How can we neglect this truth?"[24]

A highly devoted Won Buddhist laywoman in Korea in her mid-60s underwent surgery to remove a cancerous tumor. With her husband being a high-ranking public official and her son extremely successful, she received numerous visits and gifts from many people. However, as she was a mature practitioner, she was not interested in those material gifts. Instead, she called all her daughters and her daughter-in-law to come to the hospital and take the presents. However, when her daughter-in-law opened one of the gifts, the woman saw that it was a beautiful scarf in her favorite color. She imagined how perfect the scarf would look

---

23. Ibid, 291.
24. Ibid, 294-295.

if she wore it when she was released from the hospital. Just then she realized that she could not ask for the scarf back because she had already given it to her daughter-in-law. The next day, before her surgery, she was given anesthesia and briefly thought about the scarf once more. Seven hours later, after the operation was finished, she slowly came out of the anesthesia, and the first words she unconsciously said were, "Oh, where is my scarf?"

On one's death bed, one must let go of everything and focus solely on the vow of attaining Buddhahood for the benefit of all sentient beings. It is very unfortunate if one cannot let go of worries concerning work, possessions, or loved ones before one's death. Without the practice of letting go of our attachments daily, it will be hard to maintain a calm, peaceful, and focused state of mind at the end of our life.

In Korea, there is a special set of clothes called *suwee*, which is used to dress the deceased. *Suwee* is like regular clothing except for one thing: there are no pockets. There is nothing one can take when one leaves this world.

Master Chongsan said:

"There are three treasures that one should possess before the approaching nirvana. The first is charity, the second is good affinity of mutual support and the third is one pure thought. The most important of these is the one pure thought because all the charitable work one has accumulated and the many good karmic affinities one has entered, no matter how extensive, can easily be fuel for self-conceit and attachment if one has not practiced at ordinary times. What could be a greater treasure than keeping one's last one thought pure upon a thorough awakening to the principle that one comes and goes with empty hands?"[25]

Sotaesan said, "Do you know where the kingdom of Yama, the King of Death, and his messengers are? Nowhere other than inside the walls of your own house is the Kingdom of Yama. The messengers of Yama are none other than your family members. This is because ordinary people's spirits are entangled in deep, clinging affection toward their own family members in this life, and do not rise far when the body dies. Instead, their spirits fall right back toward their own previous homes. If they are not met with the opportunity to be reborn as a human being, they may be reborn as the family's domestic animal or as an insect. The buddhas and enlightened masters from ancient times emphasize the importance of developing non-discrimination, and of departing this life without attachments to avoid falling into such destinies."

"These days, people sometimes purchase a good burial plot and feel strongly that this is where they want to be buried. However, they do not realize that their spirit will go straight to that burial plot the instant they die because of their attachment to it. If in the vicinity there is not a path available to be reborn as

---

25. Ibid, 995.

a human, then they will fall unknowingly into unwholesome destinies. How could anyone be careless about this?"[26]

a) Attachment to Material Things

Spiritual practice means training one's mind, which is ultimately for attaining Buddhahood in order to free oneself from the cycle of birth and death. In one's daily life, one must be able to keep one's mind pure and clear by removing attachment to people and material possessions. It is this practice of letting go of attachments, which should be the primary focus for the achievement of liberation of mind.

Attachment means becoming bound to something or someone without being able to free oneself. When an attachment grows in our mind, our intention and interest becomes fixated, and we can no longer see things clearly or make sound judgments.

Holding an attachment while practicing towards liberation is akin to a bird trying to fly with a heavy stone attached to its wings. The weight of the stone will make it hard for the bird to fly and it will be unable to soar into the sky. However, the object of attachment, whether it is a possession or feeling toward another person, can be hard to release. Thus, liberation can be

[26]. Ibid, 294-295.

difficult to achieve.

When a rocket leaves the earth's gravitational pull, the first several miles of that journey are the most energy-consuming. It can be difficult to free ourselves from the habit energy or inertia generated by our attachment. When we are nearing death, all desires for objects, relationships, and recognition must be left behind.

When we are attached to material things, we fall into unwholesome realms of existence. When we are attached to objects we love or hate, we will also fall into unwholesome realms of existence. The same is true for attachments to religious beliefs or goodness. Even though goodness itself is very beneficial, attachment to it can create serious problems. Even the attachment to attaining great enlightenment can be an obstacle in our life if we become shackled by it.

Material things are necessary for us to live, and can enhance the quality of our daily life. These days, technological advancements and economic growth have contributed to luxurious and comfortable lifestyles. However, our desire for material possessions can be boundless. The desire to obtain more and more possessions makes us become enslaved to material things. Therefore, the possession of material things begins to overpower and dominate us. This gradually acts like a poison that slowly destroys our minds and lives.

Jesus said that just as no one can serve two masters, one cannot serve both God and money. Jesus also said, "I tell you the truth, it will be hard for a rich person to enter the kingdom of heaven! I say, it is easier for a camel to go through the eye of a needle than for a rich person to enter into the kingdom of God." (Matthew 19:16–24).

You might wonder, "If we let go of everything, how can we function in today's society?" Letting go of possessions is about releasing our attachments to them, not necessarily the possessions themselves. It doesn't mean we abandon essentials like food, shelter, or transportation. It means we shouldn't orient our lives solely around acquiring more and more material things.

As long as we remain unattached to them and use them for noble purposes, we will embody the dharma of non-possession and be able to let go of attachments.

b) Attachment to Sexual Desire

In *The Sutra of Forty-Two Sections*, Section 22 & 24, the Buddha said:

"People cling to their worldly possessions and sexual passions so blindly as to sacrifice their own lives. They are like a child who tries to eat a little honey smeared on the edge of a knife. Even though the amount is not enough to appease his appetite,

he will lick it and risk cutting his tongue in the process."
"Of all longings and desires, none is stronger than sexual desire. This passion has no equal. Fortunately, there is only one such overpowering desire. If there were another as powerful, few in the world would be able to cultivate the Way."

A lifestyle driven by lust, even within a marriage, can hinder spiritual growth. Not only can it be detrimental to one's health, but also creates attachments and binds individuals to desirous tendencies. As a result, karmic seeds are sown, and may be carried over into one's next life. The karmic repercussions of promiscuous behavior among unmarried partners are even more harmful and may yield even more serious outcomes.

There was once a man plagued by ceaseless sexual desire, and in his despair, he wished to mutilate himself. The Buddha said to him, "Mutilating your body is not as effective as purifying your mind. The mind is the leader: if the leader is restrained, its followers will also cease. If you don't rid your mind of its corrupt thoughts, what purpose does it serve to harm your own body?"

When we are seeking enlightenment, it can become a significant obstacle for us to concentrate on spiritual practice if we are unable to control sexual desire.
When energy is wasted in pursuing desires of the flesh or satisfying various desires in many forms, it diminishes our motivation to practice and weakens our original vow. It becomes

challenging to concentrate on our practice. The idea that awakening can be achieved without freeing oneself from this desire is completely misleading. That's why many Buddhist masters in the past emphasized celibacy for monastics in order to devote themselves to practice. The notion that one can overindulge in secular desires and simultaneously attain Buddhahood is a delusional idea that merely rationalizes our hidden desires. In any domain, to achieve a monumental task, one must focus one's energy. If one genuinely wants to achieve something, one should forgo what is less important.

c) Attachment to Hatred

The worst kind of attachment is that caused by hatred. Unfair treatment often creates resentment or anger. Even though one might be a devoted practitioner, such resentment or anger will not vanish easily. Practitioners should be aware that an angry or resentful mind can generate a damaging effect on one's life. Anger can transform our behavior completely. It can cause us to lose control and bring harm to both ourselves and others. Many people are afraid to contract food poisoning. Clinging to hatred or anger indicates a poisoned mind, which is something that everyone should fear much more than food poisoning. For the sake of one's peace of mind, one should maintain harmonious relationships with others by alleviating attachments to anger or hatred so one can make healthy decisions. Without applying effort, this karmic seed of attachment to hatred will persist for many lifetimes. It is important to learn to yield to others and control our anger. Master Chongsan said, "When one yields, one can cultivate virtue." Because we so habitually desire to win all the time, we often make enemies of our acquaintances.

There is a saying that goes: "The mouth is the gate of calamity." Thus, we should be especially aware of our language and use it carefully. A single thoughtless word can hurt another's self-esteem, which could damage our relationship with that person for a lifetime. We should be careful not to touch an inner wound that is hidden deep within someone's heart and mind.

There is a saying, "A stone mindlessly thrown can kill a frog." There is a Korean proverb that says, "When a woman holds resentment, frost can fall even in May." The result of holding resentment can be very powerful.

Master Jeongsan, one of Korea's greatest spiritual teachers of the 20th Century, was once offering a prayer for a grand dharma project. Absorbed in the prayer, he forgot a request from a village woman who had asked him to pray to cure her child's serious illness. Despite the Master's devoted dedication to his prayer, he struggled to direct his energy, and his prayer seemed unanswered. Suddenly, the villager's request came to his mind. He first directed his prayer toward the child; afterwards, he felt that his prayer for the project was answered as well.

It is said that the flow of heaven and earth is affected by the disturbance of even a fly's life force. However great a project might be, if the energy of one person gets in the way, the project might not be achieved. If a person holds resentment or has a poisonous mind, they will generate strong negative energy, which can seriously damage their relationships with others.

What seems trivial to one person may be of utmost importance to another. Hatred or a desire for revenge can consume the entire body and mind, leading to never-ending conflicts.

Thus, the serious negative karmic seed that we plant through anger or hatred can cause us to become shackled without hope for freedom.

We need to prepare ourselves for difficult or unreasonable situations which could arise from our past karmic debts. Each situation should be faced with sincere patience and perseverance. This is an important element of our spiritual practice as well as our life.

Seeing a disciple getting angry and suffering from another's insult, Sotaesan said, "When it is your turn to retaliate, just let it go. If you do so, the karma will come to rest. If you retaliate, the other person is bound to reciprocate and the mutual conflict and harm may never cease."[27]

Hoh-lu of Wu invaded Wueh and was defeated by Kou-

---

27. Ibid, 223.

chien, King of Wueh. Later, Hoh-lu's son, Fucha, made his bed on top of a firewood pile. Whenever people went in and out of his room, he made them shout, "Fucha, do not forget you must avenge your father." In this manner, he strengthened his desire for revenge. Having been informed of this situation, King Kou-chien attacked Wu, but this time was defeated. The king, queen, and their people became prisoners and suffered many hardships. They were released only after the king made a vow that Wueh would be a colony of Wu forever.

As soon as Kou-chien returned to his country, he had a gall bladder hung right beside his seat. Every day he tasted the bitter gall, reminding himself of the insult he had received from Fucha.

One day, he offered Fucha a beautiful woman to distract his mind, while he greatly strengthened and trained his army. Twenty years later, King Kouchien of Wueh invaded Wu. This time, Wueh defeated Wu, and it is said that Fucha killed himself.

As such, anger or hatred in one's mind is like a bomb buried in the soil. It can explode anytime, anywhere, on anyone. It inflicts harm to all those concerned.

The impact of a vengeful mind is not limited to hurting an individual. It is like a bomb that can destroy world peace. A vengeful mind eventually brings terrible retribution to one's future. Anger and resentment are detrimental to our own well-being as well as to others, and these negative emotions can also perpetuate cycles of animosity and retaliation.

The Buddha said, "Holding on to anger is like grasping a hot coal with the intent of throwing it at someone else; you are the one who gets burned."

We need to overcome these negative emotions through mindfulness and self-control, and cultivate a heart filled with love and compassion. This is the path to personal well-being as well as for the well-being of others and the greater good.

The Buddha said, "In this world, hate has never yet dispelled hate. Only love dispels hate. This is the law, ancient and inexhaustible."

The Grave Matter of Life and Death

The Buddha taught of eight kinds of suffering or dukkha. These are outlined as follows: Birth is suffering, aging is suffering, illness is suffering, death is suffering, dissociation from what is pleasant is suffering, association with what is unpleasant is suffering, not obtaining what we seek is suffering, and the scorching blaze of the five aggregates is suffering.

Birth is suffering. Have you ever seen a baby who is smiling during birth? Even when the Buddha was born, he came into this world crying, as did all saints and sages. Further, many women say that labor is the greatest pain they have ever experienced.

All our life is suffering—including anger, disappointment, depression, jealousy, and sadness—and begins with our birth.

Aging is suffering. However powerful, smart, or successful we are, we cannot avoid aging. As we grow older, we become unable physically, mentally, or emotionally to enjoy many things. In old age, we all tend to encounter unsatisfactory situations, such as being ignored and lonely, or encountering financial difficulties. We also experience decreased mental, visual, and auditory capacity. All this is unavoidable, and is suffering.

Illness is suffering. We know many people in the terminal stages of cancer and we can see how painful that is. I know one young boy who lost his hearing because a simple fever was not treated in time. In less privileged countries, many people still die because of the lack of simple medicines.

Death is suffering. One time, a woman was wailing at her late husband's funeral. She embraced his coffin and cried, "Why? Why, God? Why my husband?" Her husband had been killed in a car accident only two days before his graduation from a Christian seminary.

Some people meet a very painful death. The uncertainty, the fear, the anxiety before death—all of this is suffering.

The Buddha said, "Some people die in their mother's womb, and some die as soon as they are born; some die when they are crawling and some while walking, some are young, and some are old. Everyone disappears like the fruit that falls to the earth."

Dissociation from what is pleasant is suffering. Many people think that the greatest stress they can experience is being parted from their loved ones. The objects that we love and cherish need not necessarily be people. Losing our attractive appearance, our popularity, or our job can also be dukkha.

I heard about a woman who became obsessed with plastic surgery after her divorce. She thought her husband had been having affairs with other women because she had lost her attractive appearance. Despite many operations, she could not become as attractive as she had hoped. She eventually needed psychiatric treatment and was sent to a mental hospital.

However much we cherish something, we will eventually lose it. Reflect for a moment on what you cherish most. Impermanence is the nature of all things.

Association with what is unpleasant is suffering. There are things that we dislike but still have to encounter every day or every week. This could be a family member, our boss, or our job.

Even if we hate our jobs and are very tired, we still have to go to work every day. Even if we dislike our roommate or partner, in many cases, we still may have to live with them for a long time.

Many unavoidable situations exist that make us suffer.

'Not Obtaining What We Seek' is suffering. My friend developed colon cancer when she was in her early sixties. Despite all her efforts, ranging from a strict diet and exercise to prayer and meditation, she could not restore her health. The cancer spread to all of her internal organs. In spite of working very hard, many people cannot earn enough money to make ends meet. The inability to attain what we want—whether it is good health, success in our career or business, or something else—is suffering.

'The Scorching Blaze of the Five Aggregates' is suffering. The Buddha said the world is on fire; human minds are ablaze. We

often suffer from uncontrollable jealousy, anger, inner conflicts, bad memories, and regrets. All arise from the five aggregates: physical body, sensations, perceptions, impulses and consciousness of our body and mind. Like a moth that is so attracted to the light of a flame that it flies into the fire, we humans destroy our freedom and happiness because of mental and physical desires.[28]

These eight types of suffering have been described here in a personal way, but suffering on a global level is also boundless. Trillions of dollars are spent on many wars, and millions of children die because they cannot get clean water or simple medicine. The Buddha said that if all the tears that humans shed could be gathered, they would fill a vast ocean.

Yet, sometimes we experience pleasure and enjoy the experiences in our lives. So why did the Buddha say that life is dukkha? It is because everything is temporary; a beautiful flower withers, hair eventually turns gray, and everything that pleases us eventually passes. This is why the Buddha said, "Whatever is impermanent is dukkha." Even if everything seems perfect, the happiness that comes from our environment—that conditional happiness—is insecure, fragile, and fleeting. Only in fairy tales can one live happily ever after.

Why did the Buddha speak of these various kinds of suffering in such a specific way? He did so to convince us that the reality of suffering in our lives is unavoidable and inevitable.

---

28. Dosung Yoo, *Thunderous Silence*, 145-148.

All kinds of human suffering—whether illness or death, departing from loved ones, or not being able to obtain what we want—originate from birth; from the fact that we have human life. What the Buddha realized is that, due to our karma, which originates from ignorance, humans are driven into successive rebirths and subsequent suffering.

Therefore, the one and only way to be free from suffering is to be liberated from the cycle of birth and death. That should be the ultimate motivation of our spiritual practice.

In Korea, many people without sight live with daily difficulties that those with vision cannot imagine. Without the help of others, they need to eat rice, soup, and side dishes all from one plate, and struggle to simply go to the bathroom. Most of all, it is extremely hard for them to make financial ends meet. Some of them work as massage therapists, but many of them end up being panhandlers. They live nearby Jonggak subway station and beg for money in the subway trains, sometimes singing as they move from one subway car to the next. When they get off at stations other than Jonggak station, they often get robbed by street thugs who know that the blind beggars receive money from commuters. The blind panhandlers need someone to protect them from those thugs, but they cannot afford to hire the protection they need. Instead, they ask their children to accompany them in the subway. However, the young kids usually refuse to accompany their parents because they don't want to be seen with them by their friends. Blind parents often have to argue every morning with their children about taking the subway with them. I heard that such arguments sometimes get so heated that it becomes almost a war between the parents and their children.

Yet, perhaps equally unfortunate is the situation of the people who are not physically blind but are blind in their hearts and minds.

Jesus said, "Whoever has eyes, let them see."

Those who do not know the truth of eternal life, the truth of neither arising nor ceasing, are blind.

Sotaesan said, "The physically blind know that they are blind; however, those who cannot see with their mind do not even know that they are blind."

Ahimsaka was born into a Brahmin family in the kingdom of Kosala, India. When he was young, he was sent to study under a renowned Brahmin guru. Due to his intelligence and dedication, Ahimsaka surpassed his peers, quickly becoming his teacher's favorite pupil. This favoritism afforded him many privileges, sparking jealousy among the other students.

One day, these students deceitfully claimed that Ahimsaka was having an illicit affair with their teacher's wife. Initially, the teacher dismissed these allegations. However, upon hearing it over and over, he eventually believed them and sought revenge against Ahimsaka. Recognizing Ahimsaka's physical prowess, the teacher devised a devious plan. The teacher instructed Ahimsaka to murder a hundred people, bringing back a finger from each person as a fee for his teachings. The teacher believed that Ahimsaka would be killed during this gruesome quest.

Committed to earning his teacher's approval, the obedient Ahimsaka trusted his teacher's words and set out to fulfill this horrifying task.

Thus, he became the highway murderer, at first keeping count of the number of people that he had killed by hanging the fingers of his victims on a tree. However, when birds started to consume the fingers, he fashioned them into a string, which he wore around his neck. This morbid adornment earned him the name Angulimala, which translates to "garland of fingers."

When the king of Kosala learned of Angulimala's violent spree, he was determined to apprehend him. Hearing this, Ahimsaka's mother ventured into the forest, hoping to warn her son. By then, Angulimala had amassed ninety-nine fingers and was eager to find his final victim.

Foreseeing a looming tragedy, the Buddha decided to venture into the forest, fearing that Angulimala, in his desperation, might harm his own mother. When Angulimala spotted his mother, he hesitated. Then, seeing a monk (the Buddha) nearby, he targeted him instead. Despite his swift pursuit, Angulimala couldn't overtake the seemingly slow steps of the Buddha.

Exasperated, Angulimala yelled, "Stop, monk!" The Buddha calmly replied, "I have stopped. It's you who haven't." Confused, Angulimala demanded clarification. The Buddha explained, "I have stopped ignorance, desires, and violence, but you continue to harbor desires, anger, and commit murders. So, it is you who have not stopped."

These profound words deeply resonated with Angulimala. Recognizing the monk's wisdom and bravery, he discarded his weapon, renounced his violent ways, and joined the Buddhist order.

Before his conversion, Angulimala's mind was consumed by violence and negative thoughts. Similarly, many people are trapped in cycles of negative habits, anger, or malicious intentions. Are we so different from Angulimala?

Continuously repeating harmful patterns embodies samsara, the perpetual cycle of life and death, which leads to endless suffering. When delusive thoughts arise, we are trapped in samsara; when they dissipate, samsara ends. Samsara literally means "movement," whereas nirvana is stillness—where the flame of desire caused by ignorance is extinguished. Only when ignorance stops, does the endless cycle of birth and death disappear.

Those who achieve this liberation are termed 'arhats,' meaning "foe destroyers" in Sanskrit. This enemy is our own ignorance. Temples dedicated to the Buddha are given names such as, *daewoong-chun*, meaning 'Hall of a Great Hero,' because he conquered the enemy, which is ignorance.

Humanity's universal desire is to end suffering. Thus, what can be more imperative than breaking the shackles of ignorance and freeing ourselves from the cycle of birth and death?

In the snow-covered Himalayas, there is a bird known as *yamyungjo* (夜鳴鳥), or "nightingale" in English, renowned for its nocturnal cries. This bird is very sensitive to the cold. Legend has it that during especially cold nights, the nightingale cries out, making a promise to itself that it will build a nest the following day. However, as the sun rises and warms the air, the bird plays with its friends and forgets its promise. As night returns and temperatures drop, the bird once again cries out, vowing to build a nest the next day. Thus, the bird remains trapped in a cycle of pain and regret throughout its whole life.

We should consider whether we resemble the nightingale. As practitioners, we need to contemplate this so we can better prepare ourselves to be liberated from the cycle of birth and death.

During the filming of a social experiment, a man entered an elevator and noticed that everyone on the elevator faced the wall. After a moment's hesitation, he joined the others and also faced the wall. The man's action illustrates how we often conform to the behaviors and norms of society, regardless of whether they are beneficial or not. This demonstrates how external situations, conditions, and the opinions of others significantly influence our mindset and actions.

Dominant worldly values and external situations often dictate the course of our lives.

Practitioners should not mindlessly follow the lifestyle of the majority. Rather, as the Buddha said, they should "swim against the stream." We should not be afraid of differing from others. Tigers and eagles are solitary animals; practitioners should emulate tigers and eagles, making friends with our authentic selves, and not blindly following the herd.

> The poet Rilke wrote:
> I am too alone in the world
> And not alone enough
> To make every moment holy.

If we spend too much of our time and attention surrounded by those who are not in practice, it will be difficult to contemplate the grave matter of life and death.

If we live following the majority's value system, our final destination will be far from nirvana.

Living outside the mainstream can be difficult and sometimes painful; yet, it is far more painful to repeat the same habits and remain wandering in samsara.

Jesus said, "For my yoke is easy to bear, and my load is not hard to carry." (Matthew 11: 30), and "I have told you these things so that in me you may have peace. In the world you have trouble and suffering, but take courage—I have conquered the world." (John 16:33).

The Buddha, Sotaesan, Jesus, and other saints and sages are the ones who found the path—the way to unconditional happiness and freedom. Therefore, their dharma words should direct our value system and our lives.

When we practice the dharma to prepare for eternal life, we are like a satellite launched into the sky. At first, the satellite will have to struggle against gravity, but once it enters outer space, it orbits easily and automatically without effort.

Initially, our practice is a struggle; we must fight against our tenacious habits. As time passes, however, our practice becomes natural and effortless.

One day, a Zen master noticed a novice monk busily engaged in various tasks and neglecting to focus his time and energy on his practice. The master instructed the student to fetch a bucket and presented him with three piles: one of stones, one of gravel, and one of sand. He first instructed the novice monk to pour the sand into the bucket, followed by the gravel, and then the stones. After adding the sand and gravel, the student realized there was no space left for the stones.

The master then asked the novice monk to empty the bucket and begin again, this time placing the large stones in first, followed by the gravel, and then the sand. With this arrangement, the gravel nestled naturally among the stones, and the sand filled the spaces between the gravel and the stones.

Through this exercise, the master illustrated the importance of prioritizing tasks, emphasizing that the monk should attend to his primary practice above all else.

Verses 11 and 12 of the Dhammapada say:
Those who mistake the unessential to be

essential and the essential to be unessential,
dwelling in wrong thoughts, never attain the essential.

Those who know the essential to be
essential and the unessential to be unessential,
Dwelling in right thoughts, attain the essential.

In today's fast-paced world, most of us are perpetually busy, whether in school or at work. But it is essential to pause and consider the reasons behind our busyness. Are we busy scattering or gathering? Are we busy preparing for something that is eternal or something that will eventually crumble into dust in one morning?

We should reflect on the biggest "stones" of our lives. What is the most important thing in our life? What is our top priority?[29]

Master Chongsan said:

"A fleeting creature knows only one day, while a mantis knows but a month. Thus, the fleeting creature remains unaware of a month, and the mantis unaware of a year. Thus, deluded beings perceive only a single lifetime, oblivious to the eternal, whereas buddha and bodhisattvas, aware of eternity, plan the longest term and focus on the most fundamental matters."[30]

---

29. Ibid, 233-234,
30. *The Scripture of Wonbulkyo*, 921.

It's often said that art endures while life is fleeting. As practitioners, we must dedicate ourselves to pursuits that are everlasting. As soon as we realize that our lives are endlessly unfolding, we cannot help but practice dharma. Our understanding of eternal life is intrinsically linked to our spiritual practice. Our practice's primary objective should be liberation from the endless cycle of birth and death, as the formation of human suffering is rooted in that vicious cycle.

We, practitioners, need to reflect and realign the direction of our lives. Our life goal should extend beyond accumulating wealth, possessions, or societal accolades. The ultimate aim of our spiritual journey should be to break free from the cycle of birth and death: to walk the only sure path to end suffering. This realization will fuel our spiritual endeavors and naturally inspire us to set new life goals. Let us embark on a renewed journey, guided by true life goals and values.

Afterword

How to Use Our Mind

During medieval times, an artist set out to paint Jesus. So, he searched for the most compassionate and righteous person in his village to use as a model for his painting. Luckily, he discovered a young, healthy, and very kind looking man and finished the painting.

Years later, the artist wanted to paint Judas, who was the betrayer of Jesus. In his search for the most malevolent and deceitful individual in town, he ventured to the local prison. There, he encountered a prisoner whose face was perpetually marred by anger and resentment. The artist believed this man would make a fitting model for his painting of Judas.

However, as he began to paint, a sense of familiarity washed over him. To his astonishment, this prisoner was the same young man he had used as the model for Jesus years before. The young man had taken a dark path, which eventually led to his imprisonment. The transformation in his face and life had been profound.

This story illustrates how we can shape and direct our lives through the use of our minds. As we face various circumstances throughout our life, we can sometimes be like Jesus or like Judas. The choice depends on how we use our minds.

The essence of all the Buddha's teachings can be condensed into this one sentence: Everything is of our mind's creation. Sotaesan, the founding master of Won Buddhism, said that the essence of his teaching is about how to utilize our minds.

Several years ago, a woman was pet sitting for her friend in Philadelphia. While watching the dog, she was severely bitten. She later told her friends, "I never knew that so many people went to the emergency room for dog bites."

The reason a dog bites is simple: it is not properly "trained."
Parents of small children are well aware that untrained dogs are dangerous. They are far more dangerous than hyenas, lions or poisonous snakes because there are so many untrained dogs around us.

However, there is something which is far more dangerous than an untrained dog; it is an untrained "human mind." The Buddha said, "the most frightening and dangerous thing in this world is an untrained human mind."

All our happiness and unhappiness originate in our mind. Everyone should realize that if a carriage does not move forward, we need to encourage the horse that pulls the carriage and not the carriage itself. But when the "carriage" of our life does not move forward toward happiness, peace, and freedom of mind, many people will misplace their efforts by mistakenly pushing the carriage rather than the horse. Encouraging the horse is like working with the mind.

All practitioners must come to realize that the path to happiness lies in our "mind practice." To change our lives and our destinies, we must first focus our minds. To create change in our minds, we must attend to and train our minds well.

We sincerely hope and pray that this book helps all readers discover their true mind-nature. By disciplining and training their minds, they will realize a positive change in their lives and destinies. This is also the pathway to truthfully brighten and better our world.

BIBLIOGRAPHY

WORKS IN ENGLISH

Buswell, Robert Jr., trans. *Tracing Back the Radiance: Chinul's Korean Way of Zen.* Honolulu: University of Hawaii Press, 1991.

Chwasan. *The Principles for Training The Mind.* New York: Won Dharma Publications, 2022

Chon, Pal Khn, trans. *The Scripture of Won Buddhism.* Iksan: Won Kwang Publishing Co., 1988.

Chung, Bongkil, trans. *The Scriptures of Won Buddhism.* Honolulu: University of Hawaii Press, 2003.

Price, F., and Wong Mou-lam, trans. *The Diamond Sutra and The Sutra of Hui-Neng.* Boston: Shambhala Publications, 1990.

Red Pine. *The Heart Sutra.* Shoemaker & Hoard, an Imprint of Avalon Publishing Group, 2004.

Yoo, Dosung. *Thunderous Silence.* Boston: Wisdom Publications, 2013.

The Scriptures of Won-Buddhism. Iksan: Won Kwang Publishing Co., 2006.

WORKS IN KOREAN

All excerpts in this book were translated into English by the translators.

The Additional Discourses of Master Sotaesan. Iksan: Won Kwang Publishing Co., 1985.
The Scripture of Wonbulkyo. Iksan: Won Kwang Publishing Co., 1993.
Daesan. *The Essence of the Won Buddhist Canon*. Iksan: Won Kwang Publishing Co., 1996.
Kyongbong. *Touch the Door Latch in the Middle of the Night*. Seoul: Millahl Publications, 1989.

About the Authors

Venerable Wolsan

After Venerable Wolsan entered the Won Buddhist faith, he served as the head minister of many Won Buddhist Temples in Korea and also served on the Supreme Council. He has dedicated his whole life to making Won Buddhist teachings accessible to as many people as possible.

Venerable Wolsan has authored many books, including *Master Chongsan, The Stories of Sotaesan, The Guide for Mind Training, We Harvest What We Sow*, and *My Dream and My Life*.

Venerable Yetawon

Venerable Yetawon joined Won Buddhism in 1940 at the age of fifteen when Sotaesan, the founding master of Won Buddhism first established a practice community at the Headquarters of Won Buddhism in Iksan.

As a Won Buddhist minister, Venerable Yetawon served as a Won Buddhist minister for more than fifty years, establishing

Jungdo Retreat Center and Samdong-won Retreat Center. She is also the author of the books: *Prayer* and *Deliverance for the Deceased*.

Reverend Dosung Yoo

Reverend Dosung Yoo is a teacher and lecturer of meditation, Buddhism, and the Won Buddhist dharma in the United States and in Korea. He currently serves as the Director of the Won Dharma Center in Claverack, New York.

He is a writer, editor, and translator: the author of *Thunderous Silence: A Formula for Ending Suffering*; publisher and translator of *The Method of Sitting Meditation; Tales of a Modern Sage; The Moon Rises in Empty Space*; and *The Principles for Training the Mind,* and *The Life of Sotaesan.* .

About the Translators

Reverend Dosung Yoo

Reverend Dosung Yoo is a teacher and lecturer of meditation, Buddhism, and the Won Buddhist dharma in the United States and in Korea. He currently serves as the Director of the Won Dharma Center in Claverack, New York.

He is a writer, editor, and translator: the author of *Thunderous Silence: A Formula for Ending Suffering*, publisher and translator of *The Method of Sitting Meditation; Tales of a Modern Sage; The Moon Rises in Empty Space; The Principles for Training the Mind,* and *The Life of Sotaesan.*

Kathy Abeyatunge

Kathy Abeyatunge, dharma name Won JiYeon, joined the Won Dharma Center in Claverack, NY in 2014 and became ordained as a Lay Minister (Wonmu) on January 7, 2024.

She dedicates herself to drawing on the profound yet simple and practical teachings of Won Buddhism to spread the dharma of Timeless and Placeless meditation in daily life.

In 2024, she translated Venerable Wolsan's book into English: *The Life of Sotaesan.*